PAUSE

IN MY PRESENCE

Joshua Fowler with Zoë Fowler

"YOU WILL FIND ME IN THE MIDDLE OF THE PAUSE"
—GOD

PAUSE

IN MY PRESENCE

Advantage
BOOKS

JOSHUA FOWLER
WITH ZOË FOWLER

Table of Contents

Joshua Fowler with Zoë Fowler

What People are Saying about
Pause in My Presence!

"Written with prophetic conviction, Pause in My Presence reminds us why taking time to be still in God's presence, reflecting on Scripture and praying are non-negotiable spiritual disciplines for every believer. This book is an invitation to selah, to draw close to God and seek communion with him during a time of chaos and uncertainty."

—Samuel Rodriguez, New Season Lead Pastor
NHCLC President, Author of "You Are Next!"
Executive Producer "Breakthrough" The Movie

"Our post-modern culture has substituted activity for effectiveness. The frenzied and frantic pace of the world serves only to increase anxiety and uncertainty. Dr. Joshua Fowler's new book, Pause In My Presence, underscores the importance of waiting upon the Lord. A few moments in the secret place of His presence are far more valuable than a lifetime in the spotlight of men's attention. Dr. Fowler gives you strategies for achieving your goals more quickly--by slowing down."

—Dr. Rod Parsley
Pastor and Founder
World Harvest Church, Columbus, Ohio

In this book Joshua and Zoë help to unveil the truth and impact about Selah, pausing, waiting upon the lord. As you read this book you will not only be inspired but impacted to be one who learns to "Selah" pause in Gods presence. "But those who wait on the LORD Shall renew their strength; They shall mount up with wings like eagles, They shall run and not be weary, They shall walk and not faint." Isaiah 40:31 NKJV

—Pastor Tony G K
New Hope Revival Church, London UK

Pause in my presence is a life changing book and is one jewel of wisdom you must add to the treasure box. Every Opposition we face in life is just another opportunity to display to those around us that we have promises that can be trusted from a God who cares about every detail of our lives. Joshua Fowler truly describes the heartbeat of the father and points everyone into the direction that heals and restores in Jesus Christ. As I read this my heart was ignited. What a tremendous blessing that we serve the only God who restores, renews and gives us do overs no matter what. He isn't like people, He doesn't walk out on us when we mess up but instead, walks in. He loves to use people with the worst past to create the best futures. Pause in my presence brings you closer to this understanding. He loves us so much that there is nothing we could do more or less to have His unconditional love. This book will awaken you to all the promises that He has for you.

—RealTalkKim
Author of Shut Hell Up
RealTalkKim.com

Right now the Church is being given the opportunity to embrace a season of divine "reset," as the Holy Spirit is refreshing our perspective, renewing our vision, and restoring our strength. In this new book, Joshua Fowler highlights the immense value of cultivating a lifestyle of practicing the presence of God. In His presence is where the deepest desires of our heart and the answers to all of our prayers are found. Pause In My Presence will encourage you to seek God intently, pray prophetically, and take action accordingly. Choose today to draw closer to God and listen to what He speaks into your life. I believe you will begin to see new growth, increase, and supernatural breakthrough!

—Dr. Ché Ahn
Founder and President, Harvest International Ministry
Founding and Senior Pastor, Harvest Rock Church, Pasadena, CA
International Chancellor, Wagner University
Founder, Ché Ahn Ministries

As God's people, we sometimes get so caught up in working for Him that we forget to take time to be with Him. There is no substitute for time in the Lord's presence. In Pause in His Presence, Joshua Fowler has done a fabulous job of reminding us to examine our priorities and to keep God first. I encourage you to read this book slowly and glean everything you can from these pages. Then, as you incorporate times and seasons of selah into your own life, I know your heart will be satisfied as you grow closer to Jesus!

—Hank Kunneman
Pastor, Lord of Hosts Church
One Voice Ministries hankandbrenda.org
Host, New Level with Hank & Brenda

"Joshua Fowler has placed his finger on the pulse of what is happening in the Spirit. Pause In My Presence is a powerfully written prophetic book, that reminds us all that we are called to be Secret Place Dwellers. Joshua skillfully shows us that life is found in the pause. When we abide in the presence of God, He renews our strength and fills us with joy."

—Joshua Giles
Pastor/Founder, Kingdom Embassy
Author of "The Rise of the Micaiah Prophet"
JoshuaGiles.com

"My heart resonated positively with everything Joshua and Zoë are saying in this book. It is what the Holy Spirit is saying to the people of God today. It is all about worship, pausing to reflect on God's goodness and drawing closer to him. I deeply enjoyed studying the full meaning of the word Selah, and I was blessed to learn of all of the richness it implies. It encouraged me to spend more time reflecting on the many wonderful attributes of our God."

—Doris Wagner
Global Spheres

"Pause in My Presence will give you fresh courage and a personal renewal that will give you the faith and strength you need during challenging times."

—Cindy Jacobs
Generals International

"Everything we need, want and desire can be found in the Presence of God. Our attempts to find fulfillment, peace and security in other people, places, and things apart from God by following our own understanding and tastes will always fail. If He gave us everything we ever wanted and left us to our own devices, we would be miserable. In Pause In My Presence, Joshua and Zoë Fowler explain how we can find those things we really need in the Presence of God so that beautiful moments become a beautiful lifestyle with Jesus Christ."

—Joan Hunter
Author/Evangelist/TV Host of Miracles Happen*!*

"Make room for Jesus. Abide, be vitally united to Him. Make time to create the atmosphere for a dynamic relationship with Him. It is in the pause and selah moments where transformation occurs, prophetic vision and sight gained and destiny to possess is awakened and realized. This book is a must read for all believers. It is not just a book, it is a spiritual journey awakening places that are spiritually dry. The message scribed on these pages carries His glory and presence with keys of revelation birthed in heaven to draw you into the fullness of all He has designed in this new era. Thank you Joshua and Zoë for this now message to the Body of Christ. It is my prayer and belief that it will birth a spiritual fire, revival and spiritual awakening in this strategic time of history."

—Rebecca Greenwood
Christian Harvest Int'l
Strategic Prayer Apostolic Network

"The moment I read this book I immediately thought of Psalm 16:11 (Amp) You will show me the path of life; In Your Presence is fullness of joy, at Your right hand there are pleasures forevermore. "After God has spoken every other speaker is a late comer! The Almighty God has spoken Through his dear Servant; Apostle Joshua Fowler. 'Pause In My Presence' has said it all. Busyness does not necessarily mean impact. God has spoken and His voice is very clear and distinct. 'A word fitly spoken is like apples of gold in pictures of silver.' Proverbs 25:11 Thank you Dr. Joshua for this timely Word."

—Funke Felix-Adejumo
President, FFA MATRIX CENTRE, Nigeria

'Pause In My Presence' Unexpected impartation and a Heavenly download from beginning to an end as if it is a continuity of the Book of Revelation! As I was reading each chapter was opened heaven 3D with the power of the secrets and the truths of The Great Return. Dr. Joshua Fowler describes the powerful heavenly impact of the Inner court intimacy unlike anything I read before. It is the grand opening of Psalm 91 - dwelling of the shelter of El Shaddai - Secrets of the Secrets place when we pause. I believe as you read, pause and meditate, God's going to take you to a new dimension with Him to strengthen your core, change your atmosphere and transform your soul on a whole new divine level. Your walk with Christ is going to change beyond your expectations and your life is never going to be the same again.

—Pastor Isik Abla
TV & Social Media Evangelist & Author
Founder & President of Isik Abla Ministries and Dream Church

'Pause In My Presence' comes in a great time because there are so many distractions everywhere. It's all about GOD'S presence. Open your heart and receive all that this great book has to offer you. Dr. Joshua is a great man of GOD impacting the Nations! If there is a book to have, it's "Pause In My Presence'!

—Ricardo Duarte, Release The Fire Ministries, Portugal

It's only in the Manifest Presence of our Heavenly Father in unbroken relationship and intimacy, by the Power of His Holy Spirit, can the Revelation of Jesus Christ King of Glory be our Ultimate goal and Hope of eternal life! Our dear brother, Joshua Fowler and his daughter, Zoë have captured this mystery of Christ in a very readable way so we can in this present world experience The Manifest Presence of Holy Triune Godhead seen in Our Messiah Jesus Christ!"

—Samuel L. Brassfield
President, Harvest International Ministries, Inc.

"As I read through the pages of this book I had many occasions for some Selah (Pause and Consider) moments. It is a truly refreshing read, and if you would put the revelation in this book into practice you would experience God in some fresh, new ways. So I would like to encourage you to take your time with this book in absorbing the revelation contained therein, it will change your life."

—Michael Scantlebury
Author of over 24 books
Apostle/Senior Elder, Dominion-Life International Ministries
Vancouver, BC, Canada

"Love Love Loved, Pause In His Presence! This is the Word of the Lord that the Ekklisia needs right NOW. This book contains marching orders for those that are called out to rule and Reign! The Good News is so refreshing as Joshua expounds on now scriptures bringing our attention off of what we are going through and shifting it to who and where we are going too. Then as you are reading you can feel the Spirit of encouragement begin to envelope you as he shares stories and testimonies of learning how to REST, PAUSE AND TRUST in His Presence!Thank you, Joshua for bringing a sure word and recalibrating thoughts, filling them with Heavenly Realities, producing manifested victories!"Much Love,

—Barry C. Maracle
Apostle/Prophet, Author, International Minister, Canada

In Pause in My Presence, Dr. Joshua Fowler and Zoë expose the heart of God for His people to come to Him in a deep and abiding relationship. This book encourages us to enter a place of God's rest that will now shake the heavens and the earth. Many times we want the earth to simply respond to our prayers and hard work serving, but what needs to happen to shake the heavens and earth is we have to acquire the heart of God. This comes when we spend time in His presence and know and understand the obstacles to that relationship. For the glory to be released, we must first position ourselves to receive from His presence, and this book is a resource that will help us start this journey and to examine ourselves as carriers of His presence.

—Dr. Candice Smithyman
Host, Glory Road TV Show
Author, "Releasing Heaven"
candicesmithyman.com

"In this book, Apostle Joshua Fowler brings an ancient truth into our contemporary and busy world. And that truth is that time SPENT in God's Presence equals time SAVED from elsewhere - where we try to accomplish what can only be done through God's power and wisdom. By pausing to read, you will learn this divine rhythm and gain access to knowledge to change everything around you."

—Afrika Mhlophe
StepUp Institute Founder/Principal
Author/Bible Teacher, Port Elizabeth, South Africa
TV Host of 'Pressing Matters'

"If you are looking to learn more about the power of His presence, look no further. The Fowler family live and breathe the presence of Jesus. They have mastered the discipline of pausing in his presence, an active process that once mastered, is life changing. Allow Joshua and Zoë, in this book to teach you how to pause in his presence. You will never be the same!"

—John & Susie Bell
Healing Community Life Ministries
hclministries.com

"I met Dr. Fowler in 2017 by divine appointment, within minutes of the meeting I knew that this man had to come to our church. Little did I know that it was a setup for both me and my wife and our ministry. Over the 3 years the Lord has used his prophetic voice to launch us and the ministry we are shepherding to the next level. Dr. Fowler's voice is refined and distilled. A voice to the nations for the end times! His prophetic assignment to the church and the world is urgent and accurate. Dr. Fowler carries the prophetic mantle to raise the next generation of prophets. This part of his legacy a modern day Elijah as is evident in his biological and spiritual children. It is this father's heart in Dr, Fowler that makes this volume of work a much needed tool for the body of Christ in the present day. Pause in my Presence' couldn't have come at a better time. The entire world under lockdown, a Selah moment for every nation and race under the sun! In this book Dr. Fowler prophetically places the world's order in God's perspective and helps believers navigate the times in accordance with God's will. The world is peripheral to the church but the present day church in recent history has found itself grappling with its identity. We are often caught in the hustle and bustle of the world order, the rat race and the rumble which has threatened the very idea of Sabbath's rest at the very least. In this book Dr. Fowler awakens the church to reimagining effectiveness and productivity and helps us to look at the nitty gritties that makeup the overall worship experience. He does it with finesse and attention to detail, reigniting the fires the LORD has been rekindling in the church for generations! This book is a toolbox for the present day church on worship and order for both the priest and the prophets!"

—Lingelihle & Hlubi Jadezweni
Pastors, RUUC PE
Authors of To Find And To Keep
Port Elizabeth, South Africa

"I love Joshua Fowler's passion for the Lord and for the Body. As a prophet, he is a man of faith calling the Body to look to God's great love, care, and power in the midst of crisis. I have come to very much appreciate him and his ministry."

—Patricia King, Patriciaking.com

"Dr. Joshua Fowler is a good friend of over 20 years, we have the same spiritual father, Dr. Dan White, Sr., who was promoted to heaven a few years ago. This is an amazing book that Joshua and Zoë have written together. They are an anointed family who are truly worshippers and not just singers. This book was born out of the global pandemic, COVID 19. Pause In His Presence is all about waiting on the Lord, basking in His Presence, soaking and pausing long enough for the Lord to minister to you. In Acts 13, it is said that as they ministered to the Lord the Holy Spirit spoke. I believe as you read, minister to the Lord (worship Him), soak and take a selah (pause) to wait on the Lord that He will speak to you. Your life will never be the same. Then arise and be the awakener and revivalist He has called you to be and change the atmosphere in your home, city and nation."

—Dr. Mark R. Van Gundy
Co-founder of Revival N Nations, London, United Kingdom
Fire School of Revival & KSM Global TV

"'Pause In My Presence' is a must have in your spiritual arsenal. Housed within each chapter is an invitation from Holy Spirit to come deeper and closer to The Lord. I've had the privilege to run with Joshua & Zoë, both carry such a deep river for the presence coupled with a unique generational synergy to convey the heart of God as prophetic voices. In the hour in which we are living there is a resounding call to a generation to return to the secret place and this amazing new book 'Pause in My Presence' is a roadmap to encounter Jesus and his glorious presence like never before."

—Torrey M. Harper
Global Prayer Room- NYC
Habitation Church

In an age where the word "pause" is treated more as a derogatory remark than one of the attributes that made David a man after God's own heart, Joshua & Zoë enter with this strategic literary roadmap out of a frenetic pace and into presence. They invite the reader to embrace holy Selah moments with the Father. You'll go further than you've ever been when you pause more than you ever have. Accept the invitation from Joshua & Zoë to pause.

—Anthony & Melissa Medina
hopefires.com

Key principles of living life with the Father are revealed here by Joshua and Zoë in this book about Selah. Learn the benefits of leaning into the Father, being intentional with our listening ear. Matthew 6:6 - Close the door to release your Roar. Move into a relationship that underlines the basis of "In Him we live and move and have our being". Take time to Pause with this book. Allow it to encourage you, draw you and reveal Biblical truths in a fresh way. Your destiny is found in the intimate place with God, where His voice, His leading is uncovered for Us. This is a life changing book, so - pause, digest and grow. Thank you both for walking a walk before the Lord and for your obedience to write this book. Transformation awaits you.

—Andy & Sharron McClelland
Co-founders of Freedom Fire Ministries
Senior Leaders of Father's House, Christchurch, England

"Joshua Fowler has a genuine heart to impact the world for the Kingdom of God. 'Pause In My Presence' is a 'now' word for the church. Let God use this apostolic revelation to tune you in to hear His voice. I invite you to take a 'pause' and be transformed by the divine truths found in its pages. It's time for you to have a Selah!"

—Anna M. Aquino
Writer, Speaker, and Ninja Mom - annamaquino.com

In a world of distraction and chaos, my dear friend, Dr. Josh Fowler, has prophetically called us to pause in the presence of the Lord. It is here that a fresh word will be released to a generation of unconventional warriors, that will bring about a great awakening, the likes of which we have never seen! I challenge you, do not simply "go through this book," but let this book go through you!

— *Levi Lutz, Together In The Harvest*

Stop. Breathe. Make space. And be captivated by the precious presence of Jesus as you engage with this timely gem from Joshua Fowler. I'm reminded that in our fast paced culture that pushes for prominence, we don't necessarily need more activity for Jesus. We simply need more of Jesus. I'm pretty sure He is saying to us right now "Child, pause in my presence".

—James Beng Lee
Startup Founder & Songwriter
Global Ministry Director, RICE Movement, Australia
jamesbenglee.com

Joshua and Zoë Fowler have reminded us in a very succinct and powerful way that without pausing, in fact living in God's presence we will revert to pleasure, prosperity, performance & programs. None of which are bad in themselves, but can never replace the peace, power and prophetic insight that comes from pausing in the place of His presence, where He can position us to possess the kingdom & experience God's suddenly's and immediately's. "Sabbath rest" & 'Selah moments" slow our pace to stop, listen, hear and act on His instructions. Old Testament believers "rested from work" but we as New Testament believers "work from rest" keeping us refreshed & revived for the work God has called us to. Joshua and Zoë have written a manuscript which is much more than a book and as a Pastor I recommend it as a teaching and training resource which can help bless and instruct the local church.

—Brian Agnew
Pastor, Lisburn City Church
Founder, LCC Community Trust, Northern Ireland

Personally I have come to know the Fowlers to carry an anointing to build bridges and platforms for generations of God's people to run together for His Kingdom. This collaboration is significant in what God is doing on the earth and I believe it will also spark a unity in the body.

As the world has come to an unexpected halt to a standstill, Joshua Fowler and his daughter Zoë heard heaven on this book! 'Pause In My Presence' emanates a beautiful Godly timing. A seasoned prophet does not just hear and release a word from heaven, but also knows "when" and "how" to deliver it. This book hits it on the nail. This book creates a much needed space to "Selah".

Both authors are prophetic worshippers and it is evident, as 'Pause In My Presence' exudes a song of peace, a knowing and a trust, which gives the reader permission to enter into intimacy with God and the same revelation of the power of 'Pause In My Presence'.

—Lindy-Ann Hopley
Beautiful Witness Ministries
Capetown, South Africa
beautifulwitness.com

Acknowledgments

To my amazing parents, Dr. Charlie & Suzy Fowler- Thank you for raising me in the House of the Lord. Thank you for the many sacrifices you made to help me become the man I am today. Thank you for the legacy of love and passionate pursuit of His Presence that you continually live before me.

To my lovely wife, Lisa Fowler- Thank you for saying yes and standing by my side. Thank you for the countless hours and sleepless nights you endured as I was writing this manuscript and for the many contributions you have made for the completion of this book. Your love for me blows me away! I love you forever and a day plus 5 more minutes!

To my pretty little sister, Charm Miller, and her family- Thank you for all you do for our family and ministry to keep things moving forward. Your selfless, sacrificial support and tireless contributions behind the scenes make it possible for me to be before people to deliver the Word of the Lord. I love you forever.

To my beautiful daughter, Zoë Fowler- Thank you for taking this journey with me and helping to write this book. You are such an incredible writer and even more importantly, your life embodies the message of this book. If I know anyone who Selah's, If I know anyone who is passionate about Pausing in the Presence of God, it's you. I'm Papa Proud of you.

To my awesome Son-In-Love and Daughter, Eben & Destiny Black- Thank you for everything you both have done to make it possible for me to focus and write this book: all of the meals you both have cooked, the grocery runs, trips to the Post Office and so much more. Eben, your ability to make sense of the cover designs that I've scribbled and sent to you in the wee hours of the morning and your patience to transform them with such excellence amazes me.

To my joyful son, Benjamin Fowler- Thank you for all the hours and days you have sat quietly and patiently waiting for me to come outside and play basketball or to do something else with you. You exude such uncommon happiness and peacefulness for someone your age that it has made this process much easier and for that I'm so grateful. Now, we can play more basketball and go on some more Dad & Son Dates!

To my beloved first-born son and daughter-in-love, Hunter & Allison Fowler, and my adorable grandchildren, Isabella "Bella", Elizabeth "Ellie", & Isaac- Thank you for all of your prayers and encouragement throughout the years. I'm so proud of you and the fruit bearing lives you are living for the Lord.

To my Baby Girl, Selah Grace Fowler- You truly are a sign and wonder. Our surprise from heaven announcing a new season of restoration and revival in the earth. Everywhere you go your lifesong will release the refreshing grace of God to *Pause in His Presence.*

To My Spiritual Sons and Daughters- Thank you for your love, prayers and faithfulness. I'm honored to walk with you to establish the Kingdom of God in the nations. Together we will raise up generations of awakeners, build Presence Centers and "Awake The World".

To Our Ministry Partners- Thank you for standing with me and "Awake The World" for your prayers and support. Your faithfulness makes it possible for me to write books like these to encourage and impact countless lives and nations.

The Hall of Faith- Special Thanks to Charlie & Suzy Fowler, Bill & Joann Sarris, Ted Vickers, Tyrone & Una McFarland, Greg & Roxanne Barnard, Tony GK, Mark & Marry Van Gundy, Anna M. Aquino, Mark & Ruth Chaffin, Thomas Manton, Francina Norman, Juan & Aletha Koen, Hope D'Arcy, Rebecca Bachtel, Ralph & Shonda Anderson, Richard & Kaye Davidson, Conrad & Lana Engelbrecht, Pauline McNally, Meghan Middleton, John Ortiz, Belinda Spannigburg, for helping see this dream fulfilled.

Dedication

A Tribute to an Unknown Prophet

I would like to Dedicate this book to one of God's Generals who was a "Papa Prophet" to me. He was the first prophet the Lord brought into my life as a 15 year old teenager. I learned so much from him. This humble man wasn't called to the masses, and he never sought pulpits or platforms. This man was a Presbyterian Dentist who, through a divine encounter, answered the call to be a prophet. He would go wherever and to whomever the Lord would send him. Whether it was to a King, government official, pastor or driving 6 hours just to deliver a word to a teenager like me. This prophet would drive to the grocery store in the middle of the night, go to the aisle the Lord showed him, and wait for someone from the Lord's vision to show up. He would then deliver the word and go back home. This prophet taught me how to guard my heart. This prophet taught me by his example how to walk in humility, mercy and love. This prophet modeled racial reconciliation through the interracial marriage to his beautiful wife and help mate, Trella. This prophet modeled the love of the Father through the adoption of his beautiful biracial children. This prophet exemplified the compassion and love of The Father. Although he might not have been known by many on earth, I'm sure heaven stood at attention in honor and celebration as this prophet entered heaven. This prophet will never be forgotten, for his legacy will live on in his family and friends. By the Grace of God, I pray his prophetic DNA and legacy will live on through me. Well done, Prophet N.H. Dutton. Well done, receive your reward in the presence of the Lord. You are greatly missed!

Dr. N.H. Dutton
4/11/1945 - 7/1/2020

Joshua Fowler with Zoë Fowler

Introduction

On Table Mountain in Cape Town, South Africa, as my mission team and I paused in God's presence in prayer and worship, the Lord gave me a vision that altered the course of my life.

On a rooftop in Moscow, I began to weep for the city and could feel the heart of the Lord weeping over the nation of Russia, and how He longs to gather His people unto Himself. This encounter began with a pause that marked me forever.

On the thirteenth floor of a high-rise in Taipei, Taiwan, a prophetic dream I had received seven years prior while *Pausing in His Presence* unfolded before my eyes.

Beneath the Cristo Redentor in Rio de Janeiro, Brazil, in the midst of a time of corporate worship and prayer, I shared a prophetic vision of an eagle of breakthrough soaring over Brazil. As I spoke, a literal eagle then flew through the sky as a prophetic sign of The Word of The Lord. This sign from the Lord began with a *pause* that catapulted me into a greater place than I had ever been before.

As news began to arise of a world-wide pandemic, my family and I gathered in our living room for a time of worship, communion, and prayer. As we postured ourselves to *Pause in God's Presence*, the Word of the Lord regarding *"The Great Return"* came forth in such power that it shook me to my core.

What do all of these things have in common? They are the result of *Pausing in God's Presence*! Your destiny, calling and dreams will only come to pass when you learn how to *Pause in His Presence*! The Great Return, The Great Awakening and Revival which we have longed and prayed for will only take place as we learn both individually and corporately how to *Pause in His Presence*. Are you ready? This exciting adventure of learning how to *Pause in His Presence* is going to cause you to accelerate into new dimensions of God and soar into the suddenlies of Heaven like never before! Let's G ~ O ~ O ~ O!

The Great Return Prophecy
3/13/2020

"These are the days of The Great Return. Yes, these are the days of the Great Return. The R.O.I. The return on investment. The investment I made when I sowed my son into the earth as a seed for this harvest. These will be known as the days of the greatest harvest. These will be known as the days of The Great Return. For those who have turned from me will turn to me once again. They'll turn and come back to me. They'll turn and they'll come back to my house. These are the days, declares the Lord, of The Great Return. Days of the great harvest where sons and daughters will return to my house. The backsliders will return. The wayward ones will return. Nations will return back to the place at the foot of My cross; back to the place of worship. These are the days of The Great Return. I will have My return on My investment. The blood of My Son was not shed in vain. The seed that I sowed will bring forth a harvest. You will see it these days. These days are those days that your ancestors prayed for. These days are those days that generations before you longed, tasted, and prayed for. These days are those days that My prophets and apostles of old spoke of. These days are those days. Your days have become those days. The days that they prayed for and prophesied for. These are the days of the Great Return; The Great Outpouring. These are the days of The Great Awakening," declares the Lord.

"Nations will stand in awe of Me; whole nations will return to me. Watch and see, you'll see it in the news. They'll bow before Me. Broadcasters, Kings, Queens, President's, Prime Ministers, and ball players. For even in this hour I will cause those that are in Hollywood, those that are actors and athletes, they will pause during this time. Because they do not have time to do what they have done to cover up their nakedness. Now they will see their nakedness and they will realize the need that they have for My presence. That they can only be clothed by My presence. They can only be covered by My presence, and they will return to Me. Athletes by the scores and whole teams will return to Me. Stadiums, stadiums; the athletes who once ran across the field or court to

play ball will be some of those that will stand on the platforms who will preach, prophesy and proclaim My word. I'll take the actors from Hollywood and I'll take the singers and the entertainers and they'll stand before Me in awe, and they will entertain My presence. They will host Me. And the stars will surely bow. Yes, the stars of Hollywood will surely bow. I'll cause these things to take place from the White House to your house. A returning, a returning to Me.

Even the hardest ones, those who have resisted me. Those who call themselves atheists and agnostics and say there is no God. They will cry out to Me, says the Lord. Muslims will rip their clothes and they will cry out, "The Lord He is God." Monks and people who say they worship other gods will bow before me. This is the hour when all nations will flow to the mountain of the Lord. Hindus, people under demonic persuasions, and witches will bow on their knees. They'll say, "My son and my daughter; they need help," and they'll bring them to My church and bring them to My people. I will be the only one who can save and heal them. My presence will be the distinguishable difference. The contrast will be clear. The gray will be removed. The dark will be dark and the light will be light. And the people will run from the darkness into My light.

So shine the light and shake the salt. Speak up bold, speak up loud. Declare the things that you have both seen and heard. Do not be timid. Do not be shy. Do not be fearful. Stand up and say what I say, say. Go where I say go. The Lord would say, 'The people will hear you now. The people will draw near to you now. They just need people who have my peace. Go and bring My peace to them.'

For this is the first of many altar calls that I will call. These are My alter calls. These are my alter calls. This is the first of many in this generation that I have called like this. There will be other calls. There will be other needs that will arise and there will be other dark hours that will come, but My church will shine bright though them all. My church shall shine bright through them all. My church, not yours. Those that are mine; those that carry my presence, they will shine bright through them all.

Like the children of Israel, there will not be one sick one among you. Did I not do it for the children of Israel? Is not My Covenant a better covenant? If I could provide for them and keep them from all danger and harm, can I not do it now? Am I not God? My arm is not so short that it cannot save you. My covenant is sure. My blood will never lose its power. My word will remain. Stand on My word. Speak My word and you will see it come to pass.

For where are the John G. Lakes of the day? Where are the Smith Wigglesworths of the day? When will they arise? Will they wait for a comfortable time or will they arise in this crisis? I'm looking for prophets, apostles; I'm looking for My people to arise in this hour. Not in the time of convenience, but in a time of crisis. For those that are true leaders will arise. Where are the Kathryn Kuhlmanss of the day? Where are the Maria Woodworth-Etter of the day? Where are the Aimee Semple McPhersons of this day? Will you be one who will arise? Where are the Oral Roberts of the day? They're gone, they are with Me. You are here. Take your place. Take your place. Stop looking for another. Take your place.

This is the Elisha Generation. This is the double portion generation. I reserved the double portion for this generation. Double, Double, Double. Double what you've prayed; believed. I will do double. These things and greater. Greater than you have read about in history. Greater than you've read about in My word. These are the days of Elisha. Not just Elijah. These are the days of the double. One will chase a thousand. Two will chase ten thousand. The power of agreement. The power of your unity, The power of your coming together in worship will explode that will cause the plans of the enemy to implode. For his house is a house of cards. His house will not stand. His house is a house of sand and I will blow upon it and it will fall. His house will crumble and My house will remain. Nevertheless the foundation will stand sure. My Word will remain sure."

Chapter 1

Every Suddenly starts with a Selah
סֶלָה

I was caught up into a prophetic vision where I saw an arching circle of light that began around the throne in Heaven and continued down into the earth! This massive being told me that this circle continues, extends, and is strengthened though the worship and intercession of people on earth.

When the circle increased in strength, a being that was like an eagle with wings and the face of a man flew down. It grabbed the intersection where it entered into our realm with its talons. Then, like an atomic bomb, his entrance sent shock-waves of: awakening, revival, supernatural breakthrough, healings, miracles, signs and wonders throughout entire cities and nations. In this encounter, this heavenly being was able to ride the circuit from heaven and enter into the earth; that we help create through intercession and worship. The Lord calls them '*intercession intersections*'.

He said, "Tell My people that I will meet them at the *Intercession Intersection*. I will meet them on the corner of Worship and Intercession. Your Intercession is the Enter Section (Intersection) where I will send these Angels of Breakthrough and Awakening to assist with My move in the Earth. Wherever worship and intercession increase on earth you will see a greater manifestation of My presence," says the Lord. "When you Worship and Intercede you are literally creating a circuit for Me and My company to ride in upon," reiterated the Lord.

This profound encounter gripped my heart and catapulted me into greater depths of worship and intercession. The Lord introduced to me another revelation of worship. It is the Selah.

As I began to seek God's heart regarding *Selah*, my mind scrolled through my earliest childhood memories. I remember hearing my dad, Dr. Charlie Fowler, who has been ministering for 53 years, preach about *Selah*. I can still hear my dad say in his fire-filled Pentecostal voice, "Selah, just think of that!" He would ramp up with, "Just think of that! Just think of that! Just think of that! Think about the goodness of God! Think about the faithfulness of God!" That statement is actually one of the many meanings of *Selah*. Frequently, this word is skimmed over through the book of Psalms without a thought. However, God is awakening this word within His Bride and unveiling greater depths of it in this season.

How many times have you been in a service where someone said "Amen!" or "Hallelujah"? "Amen" and "Hallelujah" are mentioned only twenty to thirty times each in the bible, whereas *Selah* is mentioned seventy-four times! *Selah* is mentioned seventy-one times in more than 25% of the Psalms, and it is mentioned three times in Habakkuk. *Selah* is literally used three times as much!

Some Theologians believe it is a musical mark or an instruction on the reading of the text. It would be an instruction like "stop and listen." It can also be interpreted as a form of underlining or highlighting in preparation for the next paragraph. Thirty-one of the thirty-nine psalms with the caption "To the choir-master" include the word *Selah*. The phrase, "to the choir master," means "to triumph by His song." When we pour out our lives as worship and *Pause in His Presence*, we will triumph by His song that He is singing over us.

In summarization, the word "Selah" means:

- To pause
- Extol or lift up
- Stop and listen
- Instrumental interlude, praise-break
- To underline or highlight or reinforce; give emphasis to

- "Amen" or "So be it"

- To hang, measure or weigh

- Think, contemplate, meditate

From my time of study and prayer, this is the clearest and most complete definition of "Selah": *To Pause in His Presence* and lift up His Word.

Under the inspiration of the Holy Spirit, Psalmists in the Old Testament intentionally chose to place a greater reverence on certain words with the word "Selah". The Psalms were sung and read aloud accompanied by minstrels playing their instruments, then when a *Selah* would appear it would call forth an even higher expression toward these passages. The musicians knew to focus with heightened reverence on Selah scriptures. When I look into the Psalms I can envision the musicians and congregation in worship exalting the Word. As they would arrive at a *Selah*, they would be lifting it higher and higher! Like a cascading waterfall, crescendos of praise form wave after wave that lift the Word in exaltation. Then the worshipper would be lifted into higher realms and dimensions of God's presence. These one-of-a-kind moments of *Pausing in His Presence* are like spiritual highlighters that indelibly mark worshipers hearts with the truth of God's Word.

"Selah"
By: Zoë Fowler & Joshua Fowler

Selah
We will pause in Your Presence
Selah
We will wait for the moment
When you draw near
As we draw near
Running, running, I run after You
Longing, longing, my soul longs for You
Beating, beating, my heart beats for You"

Get Caught up in the Pause!

"God has a plan for His church upon earth. But alas! We too often make our plan, and we think that we know what ought to be done. We ask God first to bless our feeble efforts, instead of absolutely refusing to go unless God go before us."— Andrew Murray

Guard your heart from being caught up in the turmoils of life or the pursuit of things that will never satisfy. Get caught up in the *Pause*. Get caught up in the *Selah*! *Pause in God's Presence* and passionately lift up God's Word in your heart and soul. Then, you will be lifted up to higher heights and dimensions than you have ever been.

Wait for the Lord.

Run after the Lord.

Long for more of the Lord.

Let every beat of your heart beat for more of His presence.

Get caught up in the Divine Pause!

"This is why it is so crucial that we be all the more engaged and attentive to the truths that we have heard so that we do not drift off course." Hebrews 2:1 (TPT)

It is time for "Selah Sons" to arise that will release "Selah Sounds" and "Selah Songs". Friends, enrollment is now open and the Holy Spirit is inviting all who have ears to hear to join. Enroll now as a "Selah Student". Spend all of your days learning in the "Selah School of Worship". Live every day yielded and ready to create "Selah Sessions". Remember to give the Lord thanks for every "Selah Strategy" and all the "Selah Successes" you experience along the way. Cherish every moment and write them down in your personal journal of "Selah Stories" for your children and others to follow in your "Selah Steps". As you look back on your life, you will find that every suddenly, every strategy, every story, every step, every success and every song in your life were preceded by a *Selah*!

Don't Settle, Selah!

Recently, I was awakened with a prophetic dream in which I was preaching a message. I repeatedly proclaimed, "Don't Settle. Don't Settle. Don't Settle!" In this dream, I went on to say "Don't settle, *Selah*. Don't settle for a Big Mac when you can enjoy a big juicy steak. Don't settle for less than God's best for your life. Don't settle for stale and boring religiosity when you can have fire-filled revival. Don't settle for another sleepy church service when you can be wide awake, experiencing bright-eyed, up-close, personal and corporate encounters in His presence." If you will *Selah* and not settle, the "suddenlies of the heavenlies will overtake your realities."

Don't Sleep, Selah!

"Lest coming suddenly he find you sleeping." Mark 13:36 (NKJV)

"Then Hezekiah and all the people rejoiced that God had prepared the people, since the events took place so suddenly."
2 Chronicles 29:36 (NKJV)

We don't want to be caught sleeping when God comes suddenly! This is why Hezekiah rejoiced in 2 Chronicles 29:36. He rejoiced because the Lord had prepared him and all the people so well. This was so that when the Lord came suddenly, they were ready. Like the sons of Issachar we must have understanding of the times and seasons and seize our suddenly, *Selah* season!

"... of the sons of Issachar who had understanding of the times, to know what Israel ought to do, their chiefs were two hundred; and all their brethren were at their command;" 1 Chronicles 12:32 (NKJV)

It's time for Suddenly!
It's time for Awakening!
It's time for Revival!
It's time for Harvest!

Do you see it? Are you expecting it? Don't sleep through your suddenly! If you are sleeping, the harvest will overtake you, and you will not be able to reap it. Arise and shine; for your light has come and the glory of the Lord is risen upon you!

Don't Strive, Selah!

"So we conclude that there is still a full and complete 'rest' waiting for believers to experience. As we enter into God's faith-rest life we cease from our own works, just as God celebrates his finished works and rests in them. So then we must give our all and be eager to experience this faith-rest life, so that no one falls short by following the same pattern of doubt and unbelief."
Hebrews 4:9-11 (TPT)

There is no need for striving. Lean back and rest. *Selah.* You are a human being, not a human-doing. You were never called to do, you were called to be. One day while in a time of prayer, the Lord said, "You will find the rest when you enter into My rest." The rest of what you've been believing for is right where the Lord left it for you. It's in His rest.

I can still hear that famous radio commentator, Paul Harvey, say, "And now for the rest of the story!" Could it be that the rest of your story is waiting to unfold as you rest in His presence in your obedience to *Selah*? Hebrews 4:9-11 (TPT) calls this a "full and complete rest" and admonishes us to give our all, be eager to experience God's faith-rest life, and cease from our own works! I love the song by Christ For The Nations Worship, *"There is No Striving."*

Don't Stress, Selah!

"Complain and remain. Praise and be raised." —Joyce Meyer

"You will show me the path of life; In Your presence is fullness of joy; At Your right hand are pleasures forevermore."
Psalms 16:11 (NKJV)

"The Presence of God will not always fix your problems, but it will clarify your perspective." —Steven Furtick

"Yet, as God's servants, we prove ourselves authentic in every way. For example: We have great endurance in hardships and in persecutions. We don't lose courage in a time of stress and calamity." 2 Corinthians 6:4 (TPT)

"Pour out all your worries and stress upon him and leave them there, for he always tenderly cares for you." 1 Peter 5:7 (TPT)

We can't add an inch to our height stressing and worrying. Not long ago, in the midst of the most stressful time of my life, I heard the Lord say, "Relax, I've Got This!" Then He went on to say, "Relax, I've Got You!" This Word revolutionized every part of my life. I was pastoring in Orlando, Florida, at the time and taught a series of illustrated messages entitled, "Relax, God's Got This!" I sat down on a Tommy Bahama beach chair under an umbrella, sipped on a glass of sweet ice-tea, propped my feet up with flip-flops on and shared these refreshing life-changing truths of rest in the Lord. Over the years I've been encouraged by countless testimonies of church members who were impacted by these messages and others who've watched them on YouTube.

Jesus tenderly cares for you. Allow the depth of His love for you to wash out every worry. Allow the magnitude of His grace on your life to sweep away all fear. In Philippians 1:28, we see that our lack of fear amidst opposition is actually a clear sign of the enemy's ultimate destruction! You were made to abide and thrive!

Declare this aloud, "Stress, I command you to leave in the name of Jesus. Fear, there is no room for you in my life, in my thoughts, or in my family. I declare a drought on doubt! Jesus, come; perfect your love in me. Make me a shining, radiant expression of your victory in the earth. Amen!"

Pause In His Presence

It's time for a Selah Session!

PAUSE pages will be intentionally placed in specific parts of this book to allow you to encounter the Lord in the middle of His presence. Have an encounter in the middle of the pause. Take a few moments, or however long the Holy Spirit leads you, to reflect with Him. Let His Word to you permeate deeply into your heart. Ask Him to teach you to relax and rest in Him. God's got you!

"Whenever my busy thoughts were out of control, the soothing comfort of your presence calmed me down and overwhelmed me with delight." —Psalm 94:19 (TPT)

Selah Scriptures:

_____

_____

_____

_____

_____

_____

_____

_____

_____

_____

Pause Prayers:

_____

_____

_____

_____

_____

_____

_____

_____

Pause Promises & Prophecies:

_____

_____

_____

_____

_____

_____

_____

_____

Selah Reflections:

_____

_____

_____

_____

_____

_____

_____

_____

_____

_____

_____

_____

_____

_____

_____

_____

Chapter 2

Selah's Birth Twins

Suddenly & Immediately

Something phenomenal happens when you *Selah*. *Selah* births suddenly and immediately. It is in the *Selah* that you are given access to places where you once were denied. Things you prayed about for years will suddenly come to fruition, and your destiny will accelerate at a supernatural rate. *Selahs* usher in God's goodness and mercy that will overtake your life. I call this phenomenon of acceleration; God's time twins!

While ministering in Santa Rosa Beach, Florida at Christian International in 1997, the Spirit of the Lord came upon me and I prophesied that my wife would give birth in 1998 as a sign of the harvest. I was preaching on Elisha's Double Portion when this word came forth, so I should have known we would have twins! On 9-8-98, September 8th, 1998, the Lord blessed us with the birth of my beautiful twin daughters, Destiny & Zoë.

The same day my twins were born the Lord said, "Do you know that I have twins?"

I responded, "You have twins?"

He said, "Yes! Their names are *Suddenly* and *Immediately*." *Suddenly* and *Immediately* are God's Time Twins and they were created by Him to assist you in your destiny and kingdom advancement on Earth.

Golden Keys Raining from Heaven

One night several years ago as I was going through the darkest season of my life. I was awakened by the presence of the Lord. He walked into my room and lifted me into another realm where I saw golden keys raining down from Heaven to the Earth. He said He was giving keys that would bring *entrance* and *access* for the Body of Christ to enter into new dimensions. He went on to say that *Suddenly* and *Immediately* were coming. However, he told me that this time they weren't coming for a visit. They were coming to stay. During this encounter, the Lord revealed to me that Donald Trump would be our next President. He revealed to me that Donald Trump would give access to prophets and leaders to the White House. He went on to reveal to me how President Trump would receive wisdom and counsel from prophets and leaders which would give entrance and access for full-blown awakening in America and the nations. At this time, there were 17 Republican candidates running for the nomination. Several prophets and leaders that I know are frequently invited by President Trump to the White House for prayer and council. This is fulfillment! The Word of the Lord came to pass and will continue to manifest itself today.

After this encounter, I felt impressed to read a few passages of scripture, some of which I have read and preached from countless times since then. However, this time the Word became superimposed with such illumination from the Holy Spirit that it was as if I was able to see it in both HD and 3D!

The Day of the Almond is Here!

"Moreover the word of the Lord came unto me, saying, Jeremiah, what seest thou? And I said, I see a rod of an almond tree. Then said the Lord unto me, Thou hast well seen: for I will hasten my word to perform it." Jeremiah 1:11-12 (KJV)

"Now it came to pass on the next day that Moses went into the tabernacle of witness, and behold, the rod of Aaron, of the house of Levi, had sprouted and put forth buds, had produced blossoms and yielded ripe almonds." Numbers 17:8 (NKJV)

When I was reading Jeremiah 1:11, "the Almond Branch" leapt off the page, which led me on an exciting time of research. This subsequently led me to Numbers 17:8! Having preached and written about *suddenly* and *immediately* for over 20 years, I was blown away by the fact that I had never seen this before! Don't you love how the Word of God is a feast where we can discover new mysteries every day?

The word "almond" is the Hebrew word *shâkêd*, which comes from the root word to "watch" or "wake." There is a play on words in the Scriptures regarding the use of "almond" and God's "watchfulness" and "faithfulness.""Almond" means "the wakeful tree." It was the watcher, the tree that "hastens to awake" (*shâkêd*) out of its wintry sleep. This expresses the divine haste which would not without cause delay the fulfilment of its gracious promise. However, it would make it bud, blossom, and bear fruit. It also means to hasten, hastner, and sudden!

The almond tree is actually the first tree to blossom in Israel! Almonds are a sign that winter is coming to an end. It literally means *sudden awakening* and *sudden harvest* are on the way. To sum it up, the almond tree represents acceleration! Thus the almond is prophesying *sudden awakening*!

I prophesy to you that your winter season has come to an end and the day of the almond, yes, *a suddenly season*, is breaking forth in your life. You are leaving the dry and cold season of hardship and coming into the bright and glorious days of harvest. It's time for us to arise as harvesters to gather the greatest harvest of all time. A season of acceleration is dawning over America, the nations, and over you!

3 Seasons in 1 Night!

"Suddenly, God, you floodlight my life; I'm blazing with glory, God's glory! I smash the bands of marauders, I vault the highest fences." Psalm 18:28 (MSG)

In Numbers 17:8, there are three seasons that came forth from the rod of Aaron the Prophet in one night. In less than 24 hours everything shifted. Are you in need of a 24 hour turn-around? If so, get ready. It's on the way! Can you imagine it? Each of the Tribal Elders at the command of the Lord through His servant, Moses, placed their rods before the Ark of the Covenant. When they came back the next day an uncommon breakthrough had taken place.

What was the difference between Aaron's rod and the rest of the rods? What caused Aaron's rod to bring forth almonds? The rod of Aaron which was a dead stick became fruitful and brought forth almonds. Why? Because this dead stick had been in the hand of the High Priest and Prophet Aaron. This rod remained beneath the prophetic words that flowed from the prophet's lips every day. So it is when you submit to the hand of God; the five-fold leadership that God brings into your life. So it is when you remain under the prophetic word of those God joins you to. Just like this dead stick, you will see the resurrection power of God manifest in your life bringing forth sudden awakening and harvest.

The prophetic ministry coupled with *Pausing in the Presence of God* overnight transformed Aaron's rod into a life-giving, fruit-bearing tree. So it will be in your life as you align apostolically and prophetically and *Pause in the Presence* of the Lord. When you read this passage you see the rod sprouted and put forth buds, produced blossoms, and yielded ripe almonds. Notice these almonds were ripe and ready for harvest. Are you ready for your Ripe Season? If so, get connected to God's prophets and *Pause in His Presence*!

One day the Lord led me to go to the store and buy some almonds as a prophetic act. As I held the almond in my hand, I heard the Lord say to me to take it in with all 5 of my senses.

1. Look at the Almond

As I looked at that almond, I heard the Lord say, "You must see it with the eyes of faith!" This is a prophetic moment! Your suddenly **is** here!

2. Feel the Almond!

He said, "The Kingdom of God is at hand!" (Mark 1:15) Reach out into your suddenly season. Sudden awakening and harvest are not only at hand they are in your hand.

3. Smell the Almond!

Have you ever felt cut down like a stump? I have. That's the way I was feeling when God told me to smell the almond. As I smelled the almond, He said, "Just like you can smell the rain before you see it, breathe it in for I'm restoring you." Can you smell the rain? The rain of restoration is coming upon you now. Then he led me to read the following passage:

> *"For there is hope for a tree, If it is cut down, that it will sprout again, And that its tender shoots will not cease. Though its root may grow old in the earth, And its stump may die in the ground, Yet at the scent of water it will bud And bring forth branches like a plant." Job 14:7-9 (NKJV)*

4. Listen to the almond!

As I took it close to my ear I could hear Him say, "This almond has been prophesying to you since you took it in your hand." He went on to remind me that faith comes by hearing and hearing by His Word! (Romans 10:17)

5. Taste the almond!

Then God said, "Taste the almond." When I did, He said, "The Word is near you, even in your mouth!" (Romans 10:8) He went on to say to me that this is how close you are to suddenly. This is how close you are to *Sudden Awakening*. This is how close you are to *Sudden Harvest*. This is how close you are to *Sudden Revival*. He said, "It's in you!" You are a carrier of the *Suddenly*. You are a carrier of *Sudden Awakening, Revival* and *Harvest*. "Everywhere you go you will release *My Suddenlie*s and *Immediatelies*, says the Lord." Glorrrrrryyyy! Now, we invite you to partake in this powerful prophetic act in your home! Buy almonds and watch as they prophesy to you that your suddenly is here!

About This Time Tomorrow

"Then Elisha said, 'Hear the word of the Lord. Thus says the Lord: "Tomorrow about this time a seah of fine flour shall be sold for a shekel, and two seahs of barley for a shekel, at the gate of Samaria.'" 2 Kings 7:1 (NKJV)

In 2 Kings 6, we read an absolutely horrifying story where such poverty and famine was in the land that people were eating their own children. It's hard to fathom such hopelessness and despair. In the midst of all this poverty and difficulty, the prophet Elisha prophesied that "about this time tomor-row" things would not be the same. He told the people to get ready, because things were going to turn around! They were going to move from poverty to prosperity; from lack to abundance!

Like many religious people of our day, there was an unbelieving believer in the midst who expressed his feelings of doubt and unbelief. The prophet told him, "You will see it, but you won't receive it." The Word of the Lord spoken through the prophet came to pass, and they experienced a breakthrough at the same time on the next day! What happened to the unbelieving believer? He saw the fulfillment of the word, but he did not partake of it.

"Now the king had appointed the officer on whose hand he leaned to have charge of the gate. But the people trampled him in the gate, and he died, just as the man of God had said, who spoke when the king came down to him. So it happened just as the man of God had spoken to the king, saying, 'Two seahs of barley for a shekel, and a seah of fine flour for a shekel, shall be sold tomorrow about this time in the gate of Samaria.' Then that officer had answered the man of God, and said, 'Now look, if the Lord would make windows in heaven, could such a thing be?' And he had said, 'In fact, you shall see it with your eyes, but you shall not eat of it.' And so it happened to him, for the people trampled him in the gate, and he died." 2 Kings 7:17-20 (NKJV)

If you desire to partake of the promises of God, then you must believe God and those He sends into your life. We see God's 20/20 plan for our lives in His Word.

"Believe in the LORD your God, so shall you be established; believe his prophets, so shall you prosper."
2 Chronicles 20:20 (NKJV)

When we believe God's prophets, we will prosper. There are too many "non-prophet" organizations in the Church today! Because they are "non-prophet", they are non-profit. They profit little for the kingdom of God because they won't receive God's apostles and prophets. Let's be like those in 2 Kings 7 who believed and then we will enter into the dimension called, "About this time tomorrow!"

It's N.O.W. Time! = New Open Windows

What time is it? It's always now! It's NOW Time. Your next is now. The Lord once said to me N.O.W. = New Open Windows! I declare your next is now and your now is here! I prophecy *New Open Windows* are opening over your life. *New Open Windows* of opportunity, favor, and provision! *New Open Windows* of Heaven are pouring out supernatural signs and wonders over the nations now in Jesus' name. Stop saying, "Someday. Maybe someday." Or "One day I will…" Receive it today! Your some days are becoming todays. Your shall-bes are becoming realities as you *Selah*!

"You will arise and have mercy on Zion; For the time to favor her,"
Yes, the set time has come. Psalms 102:13 (NKJV)

"As you look around right now, wouldn't you say that in about four months it will be time to harvest? Well, I'm telling you to open your eyes and take a good look at what's right in front of you. These Samaritan fields are ripe. It's harvest time!"
John 4:35 (NKJV)

"And do this, knowing the time, that now it is high time to awake out of sleep; for now our salvation is nearer than when we first believed. The night is far spent, the day is at hand. Therefore let us cast off the works of darkness, and let us put on the armor of light." Romans 13:11-12 (NKJV)

Your Suddenly Season is Here!

"Yes indeed, it won't be long now." God's Decree. "Things are going to happen so fast your head will swim, one thing fast on the heels of the other. You won't be able to keep up. Everything will be happening at once—and everywhere you look, blessings! Blessings like wine pouring off the mountains and hills." Amos 9:13 (MSG)

Suddenly and *immediately* are coming to a city near you! *Suddenly* and *immediately* are coming to live with some of you! As Bishop T.D. Jakes says, "Get Ready, Get Ready, Get Ready!" Things are going to happen so fast your head will swim! Now is the time. Your *suddenly* season is here! *Pause in His presence* and you will accelerate *suddenly*.

Synergy Releases Suddenlies

"When the Day of Pentecost had fully come, they were all with one accord in one place. And suddenly there came a sound from heaven, as of a rushing mighty wind, and it filled the whole house where they were sitting." Acts 2:1-2 (NKJV)

These verses in Acts give us a prerequisite for a suddenly. You have to be in one accord and in one place. In other words, synergy releases suddenlies. Everybody wants to go their own way, do their own thing, and have an independent spirit. Then they wonder why they're not getting anywhere fast. If you want a suddenly, you have to have synergy.

Prophecy is fulfilled at a rapid rate of accelera-tion when you're in one accord and in one place. When prophecy is fulfilled, people get saved! At Pentecost, three thousand were saved. When you get in one accord and in one place, God brings a suddenly that brings forth a harvest of souls. There is an acceleration in the growth of the kingdom of God.

Disobedience Delays

You may be thinking, "Well Joshua, you haven't been through anything. Everything goes all right for you. You don't have any problems. You just write books, preach, and people get all excited. They give you lots of money." Yea, right! Angels dress me every morning too. This is what happens when you're a preacher. People don't think you have any problems or needs. They don't believe you've had to live what you're preaching. Well, I have been through some things, and I can tell you what *not* to do.

Once, in the midst of financial hardship, the provision came in late. Somebody sent the money after the deadline and I experienced heartbreaking loss. In frustration I said, "God, why didn't You show up three days ago?" Have you ever been there? That's when the Holy Spirit revealed to me an important truth. Dis-obedience delays *suddenly* and *immediately*. There were things that God had told me to do, but for whatever reason, I delayed in doing them. My delays in obedience caused delays in obedience in others. The Lord showed me that there were several people He had tapped on the shoulder and asked to sow into our ministry, but they didn't do it. Because I wasn't obedient to do something for somebody else, those who were supposed to do some-thing for me didn't do it.

You Reap What You Sow!

I decided that from that point on if God told us to do something we were going to do it right then! If He woke us up in the middle of the night and told us to give someone a hundred dollars, we would go to their house that night. Why? Because we wanted to move into a *suddenly* and *immediately* season. We were tired of delays. When He leads my wife and I to sow today, we will sow it digitally and do so immediately through the internet and apps such as Paypal, Cashapp, and so forth. I can't tell you how many times our swift obedience has resulted in a sudden harvest!

Are you tired of your *suddenly* and *immediately* being delayed? If God tells you to do something, don't sit there and hesitate for weeks and months. Do it now! You will see how *suddenlies* and *immediatelies* will overtake you.

Delay Is Not Denial

God is so aware of all of His children! He considers every sigh and is intimately aware of our every need. As we walk in obedience and wait on Him, we can walk confidently in the truth that He is taking care of every detail and every desire. If you miss the mark and delay in your obedience, don't give up. Turn your heart to the Lord in humility, repent, and go do the last thing He asked you to do. Delay is not denial! Maybe the delay has nothing to do with a delay in your obedience. Sometimes it is a matter of pressing through when the enemy tries to thwart God's plan for your life. Regardless of the case, know this; delay is not denial, for the promises of God are yes and amen. The promises of God will manifest as we persevere, praise, and *Pause in His Presence.*

From Delay Drive to I320

"Now to Him Who, by (in consequence of) the [action of His] power that is at work within us, is able to [carry out His purpose and] do superabundantly, far over and above all that we [dare] ask or think [infinitely beyond our highest prayers, desires, thoughts, hopes, or dreams]" Ephesians 3:20 (AMP)

"Never doubt God's mighty power to work in you and accomplish all this. He will achieve infinitely more than your greatest request, your most unbelievable dream, and exceed your wildest imagination! He will outdo them all, for his miraculous power constantly energizes you." Eph 3:20 (TPT)

Not long ago, I was caught up in a prophetic encounter with the Lord and He showed me a *Heavenly Super Highway* called I320. He said, "I'm moving you from Delay Drive to I320 and now you will live on Epehsians 3:20!" I have experienced fulfillment of this Word since that day. I prophesy you too are moving from Delay Drive to Ephesians 320 in Jesus name. I declare and decree over your life, family, city and nation:

- Sudden Shifts

- Sudden Strategies

- Sudden Connections

- Sudden Breakthroughs

- Sudden Signs & Wonders

- Sudden Healings & Miracles

- Sudden Awakening

- Sudden Revival

- Sudden Harvest

"And the word of the Lord came to me, saying, "Son of man, what is this proverb that you people have about the land of Israel, which says, 'The days are prolonged, and every vision fails'? Tell them therefore, 'Thus says the Lord God: "I will lay this proverb to rest, and they shall no more use it as a proverb in Israel." ' But say to them, ' "The days are at hand, and the fulfillment of every vision. For no more shall there be any false vision or flattering divination within the house of Israel. For I am the Lord. I speak, and the word which I speak will come to pass; it will no more be postponed; for in your days, O rebellious house, I will say the word and perform it," says the Lord God.' "Again the word of the Lord came to me, saying, "Son of man, look, the house of Israel is saying, 'The vision that he sees is for many days from now, and he prophesies of times far off.' Therefore say to them, 'Thus says the Lord God: "None of

My words will be postponed any more, but the word which I speak will be done," says the Lord God.' " Ezekiel 12:21-28 (NKJV)

Suddenly and Immediately Scriptures

"Suddenly" is found 71 times in the Bible and "Immediately" is found 109 times in the Bible! The following are some that I have highlighted that will strengthen your faith:

- Suddenly God Appeared! (He will appear for you Suddenly!) Numbers 12:4

- Suddenly the Glory appeared. (Get ready for His glory to appear suddenly) Numbers 16:42

- Suddenly the bones came together, none to bone! (Things are coming together!) Ezekiel 37:7

- Suddenly a woman with an issue of blood! (Issues are being healed suddenly!) Matthew 9:20

- Suddenly there came a sound from heaven! (Sudden sounds from Heaven) Acts 2:2

- Suddenly I did them, and they came to pass. (It will come to pass!) Isaiah 48:3

- Suddenly there was an earthquake & immediately the prison doors opened! (Open doors!) Acts 16:26

- Immediately I was in the spirit! (Get ready for immediate translations!) Revelations 4:2

- Zion gave birth suddenly! (Now is the time of manifestation and birthing!). Isaiah 66:7-9 (TPT)

- Suddenly your healing will manifest! (Healing is yours in Jesus' name!) Isaiah 58:6-14 (TPT)

- Suddenly it's spring! (This is your season of blooming!) Psalm 147:12 (MSG)

Chapter 3

You'll find Me in the Middle of The Pause!

"If your presence doesn't take the lead here, call this trip off right now" Exodus 33:15a (MSG)

As we entered into 2019, I heard the Lord say, "You will find Me in the waiting." Then, in August of 2019, while ministering at Christ for the Nations Institute in Dallas, Texas, I prophesied "You will find Me in the middle of the pause!" Who would have known just how profound and prophetic these words would be as we find ourselves several months in the midst of a Global Pandemic. Many of us are finding the Lord in a deeper and more meaningful way in the midst of this *Pause*. Some just wish things would go back to normal and others are saying this is a new normal. I believe there's truth to be found on both sides of the spectrum. Although I believe that this too shall pass and things will return to some sense of normal, I feel a stirring in my spirit that we must not return to business as usual. We must learn to continually find Him in the middle of the *Pause*. This is one New Norm that is not only acceptable, it's a prerequisite and priority for the life of every sincere God-lover. This must become our way of life. *Pausing in His Presence* has to become more than an every once in a blue moon kind of thing, it must be our lifestyle.

"We rarely think of the air we breathe, yet it is in us and around us all the time. In similar fashion, the presence of God penetrates us, is all around us, and is always embracing us." —Thomas Keating

A prayer of mine since the day I dedicated my life to the Lord on December 15th, 1987, has been, "Lord, I refuse to go anywhere if Your presence isn't there. I refuse to go to church for a personality. I refuse to go to church for a status. I long to be where Your presence is. I am desperate to be where Your Glory is!" Does this prayer resound in your heart, too? Are you consumed with a zeal for God's house? Does your heart burn with a longing for more?

Imagine this: you are a server tending a table. A man with kind eyes, a warm smile, and a strong, yet gentle stature sits at a table. Quickly, you rush to the table and ask, "Sir, what can I get you to drink?"

You've been running.
You've been serving.
You've been preparing.
You've been cleaning.
You've been, well: busy.

This man replies in a way that you have never heard before. The man looks deeply into your eyes and says, "Come, sit with me. I came not for you just to serve me, I came today with one desire and one intention: that you would sit with me and enjoy fellowship." At first, you are in shock. How dare this man ask me to stop what I'm doing? I'm trying to make money. I'm trying to provide for my family. I'm trying to take care of *other guests.*

This is more than a small fictional story; this is reality. Jesus rejoices in all that You do for His glory, for your family, and for others. He is incredibly proud of you. However, this Man, Jesus, has come to interrupt the busyness of your life and He's sitting at your table saying, "Friend, abide in Me. I don't want you to work for Me, I want you to rest in Me, and work *with* Me."

Maximum fruit, production, and manifestation flow from union with Jesus Christ. The ebb and flow of life comes with a hidden agenda to distract us from where our true strength and fulfillment come from: *Pausing in His presence.* Will you say "yes" to *Pause* in the middle of His presence? Will you say "yes" to the *Selah*?

"The King, full of mercy and goodness, very far from chastising me, embraces me with love, makes me eat at His table, serves me with His own hands, gives me the key of His treasures; He converses and delights Himself with me incessantly, in a thousand and a thousand ways, and treats me in all respects as His favorite. It is thus I consider myself from time to time in His holy presence." — Brother Lawrence, The Practice of the Presence of God

The Pause Prophecy 3/29/2020

I heard the Lord say, "I'm adding length of days for many of my leaders and people during this time. For what some would say is a loss of time and momentum, is really a redemption of time and momentum.

For there are some of my servants who have not known how to rest. Some who have forsaken my sabbaths. And some who've not taken sabbaticals when I've said they've needed to rest. So in this time, yes this redemption of time, I'm giving my body time to take back what has been stolen or lost. The plans of the enemy to take out many leaders and people prematurely will be foiled.

So don't let this time just pass you by then go back to business as usual when you are released. Use this time wisely to take back your health. Use this time for true riches and wealth. Yes, use this time to take back your families. Use this time to build and rebuild relationships with your companions and children. Use this time to be in My word. Use this time to do both what you've seen & heard. Use this time to rest in Me. But most of all use this time to worship me. Yes, Use this time just to come and sit at my feet.

Remember the Best Part, Yes the Best Part. It's not found in doing the Work, the best part is only found when you remember to remember by sitting at my feet. So return to me, return to my table, come commune with me and I'll make you able to overcome every sickness, ailment and disease, yes I'll cause you to preempt the plans of the enemy.

Get caught up in the pause, yes caught up in the pause. As you get caught up in the pause of my presence, that which has been lost and stolen will be caught up. Get caught up in my pause then wherever you are lacking will be caught up. Rest will be caught up, health will be caught up, time will be caught up, relationships will be caught up. You'll find in the end that even your finances will be caught up and I'll exceed your dreams and expectations.

What some call a recession, I call recess for my leaders and people. As you are on this divine recess, enter my rest then you'll receive the rest of what you need for the days ahead. For in so doing this recess will become a reset which will give birth to great healing and restoration for many!"

Pause In His Presence

It's time for a Selah Session!

*"Quiet your heart in his presence and pray; keep hope alive as you
long for God to come through for you. And don't think for a moment
that the wicked in their prosperity are better off than you."*
Psalm 37:7 (TPT)

Selah Scriptures:

_____

_____

_____

_____

_____

Pause Prayers:

_____

_____

_____

_____

_____

_____

Pause Promises & Prophecies:

_____

_____

_____

_____

_____

_____

_____

Selah Reflections:

_____

_____

_____

_____

_____

_____

_____

_____

_____

Purpose of the Pause

"There is no life outside of the presence of the Holy Spirit."
—Todd White

Have you ever been watching a movie and the screen comes to a sudden pause? You squint your eyes at the screen and read with great frustration, "Loading." Our immediate response typically is to press play a million times until hopefully it works.

However, the sudden pause is often with great intention. There are several possible reasons for the pause:

1. The TV has disconnected from the internet. There may be a possible need to recalibrate or reset the TV so it is in sync, and ready to receive the direct transfer from the transmitter.

2. The rest of the movie is still loading, and though you can force it to play, it will be of lesser quality if you were unwilling to pause for it to load.

3. The TV or internet system is out of date, and it's time to update and upgrade.

4. In addition to these possibilities, there are times that we as the person watching choose to pause the movie. There are several possible reasons for this, as well:

   a) We're hungry! The pause is an invitation to eat.

   b) Someone calls us! The pause is a time to clearly communicate with those around us.

   c) Bathroom break! The pause is an invitation to get rid of waste.

Regardless of the reason, the pause is with great intention. Let's explore these two sides of this spectrum of the pause.

The pause is a time to reset, reload, and reform.

God will reset the clock, reset the dream, and reset your mindset. Years that the enemy attempted to steal are restored in the pause. Dreams the enemy tried to steal are revived in the pause. Every dream, purpose, and plan the Lord set to accomplish in your life will come to pass.

Several years ago, I was in the most difficult season of my life. My whole life was upside down and I was absolutely broken. Every day for seven months, I wept like a baby. I clung to Hebrews 6:9a, "We have this hope as an anchor for the soul, firm and secure."

It was during that season, I experienced the presence of God so tangibly in the pause. When everything I had ever known came to a stop, God met me right there in the middle of my pause. The enemy will try to send delay, denial, and destruction, but God will meet you right where you are, pick you up out of the miry clay and set your feet on solid ground. I stand today as a living testimony of God's faithfulness to enter into the pause. God will send a divine reset into His timing, reload you with strength and hope, and reform what was old and out-of-date, to bring you into the new, fresh things He has in store for your life.

> *"For I am about to do something new. See, I have already begun! Do you not see it? I will make a pathway through the wilderness. I will create rivers in the dry wasteland." Isaiah 43:19 (NLT)*

The pause is a time to consume, communicate, and cleanse!

The pause is an invitation to feast on Jesus, His Word, and heavenly realities. John 6:35 says, "Then Jesus declared, 'I am the bread of life. Whoever comes to me will never go hungry, and whoever believes in me will never be thirsty.'" When we are hungry, we must run to the only One who can satisfy. Seeking fulfillment and fullness in entertainment, food, people, or your job will never fill you. Run to consume and commune with Jesus in the secret place. He is true bread; the source of sustenance, strength, and satisfaction.

"The law from Your mouth is better to me than thousands of gold and silver pieces." Psalm 119:72 (AMP)

"This Book of the Law shall not depart from your mouth, but you shall read [and meditate on] it day and night, so that you may be careful to do [everything] in accordance with all that is written in it; for then you will make your way prosperous, and then you will be successful." Joshua 1:8 (AMP)

"Yes, feast on all the treasures of the heavenly realm and fill your *thoughts with heavenly realities, and not with the distractions of the natural realm." Colossians 3:2 (TPT)*

The pause is a time ordained to communicate and strengthen relationships. Don't isolate yourself in the pause! Take hands with friends, family, and ministry partners. Communicating ushers in unity. There are personal, private *selah's* and corporate *selah's*. Both are needed and both will release God's heart in the earth. The heart of God is for family!

"Behold, how good and how pleasant it is for brethren to dwell together in unity!" Psalm 133:1 (NKJV)

"Let the word of Christ dwell in you richly, teaching and admonishing one another in all wisdom, singing psalms and hymns and spiritual songs, with thankfulness in your hearts to God." Colossians 3:16 (ESV)

The pause is a time to invite the Holy Spirit to examine your heart and cleanse you. As the noises of life come to a halt and you come away with the Lord, you will hear His voice with great clarity. The Word of the Lord is encouraging and edifying, but it also comes to prune, cleanse, and renew. Yield your life, routine, schedule, and habits to the Lord. Allow Him to show you a more excellent way!

"Search me, O God, and know my heart! Try me and know my thoughts! And see if there be any grievous way in me, and lead me in the way everlasting!" Psalm 139:23-24

"Every branch in Me that does not bear fruit He takes away; and every branch that bears fruit He prunes, that it may bear more fruit." John 15:2

This is God's heart for you in *the pause*. He will **reset** your life into proper alignment with His purpose. He will **reload** your system so you are full and ready to display His glory. He will **reform** the old system and accelerate you into the new thing. Then, get ready to **consume** His Word, **communicate** with others, and be **cleansed** in God's presence!

The Pause Game-Plan!

"It is in recognizing the actual presence of God that we find prayer no longer a chore, but a supreme delight." —James Gordon Lindsay

Taking time to pause can range anywhere from a minute at a red light to hours in the secret place. The whole purpose of it is to realign your heart and posture yourself toward the face of Jesus. Seconds, minutes, or hours, the amount of time isn't what is most important. What is most important is that each and every *Selah* creates a deeper place of communion with Jesus and awareness to His Spirit. It's not how long you pray, it's how long you go without praying! Smith Wigglesworth said, "I don't often spend more than half an hour in prayer - but I never go more than half an hour without praying."

"Your future is found in your daily routine. Successful people do daily what others do occasionally! "— Paula White

Pause Game Plan & Pointers (Daily Routine)

- Pause first thing when you wake up and last thing before you go to sleep.

- Pause at traffic lights, during commercials, and while getting dressed.

- Pause 7x's a day. *"I stop to praise you seven times a day." Psalm 119:164 (TPT)*

- Pause at least every 2-3 hours.

- Set alarms on your phone to Pause in His Presence.

- Doctors recommend that we drink 1/2 our weight in water daily. (Water is worship!)

- Start with pausing for 2-5 minutes, then increase the time as you grow!

The Power of the Pause

Since I was a kid, I have always loved basketball! I remember when I was 5 years old. I would play hours and hours every day working to increase my speed and perfect my shot. I even set the state record in Florida for the most 3-pointers in a game. In the game of basketball, if you're fouled by your opponent while shooting, you will hear the sweet sound of the ref's whistle blowing, signaling your way to the free-throw line. This free-throw line is a place of great joy for great shooters because it can mean free points! My routine at the free-throw line has always been to spin the ball, dribble twice, spin the ball, dribble twice, *pause*, and then shoot! The most important part of this moment is the *pause*. It's a time to collect thoughts and position yourself to make a goal! Time and time again, right after pausing, I would hear the sound of the ball floating right into the net: swoosh! What a sound!

Pausing will always help you accomplish your goals! If I had just been fouled by an opponent and approached the free-throw line, and rushed to shoot the ball, I probably would be out of breath, out of form, and my vision would be out of alignment. But pausing will restore your breath and position you into proper alignment. It will help you to see with clarity. Make pausing a part of your daily game-plan. First, try to integrate it with a few alarms on your phone, or specific times of the day. Then watch and see as you will begin to hear God's voice with more clarity than ever before!

I learned that in order to score: I would have to fake like I was going to shoot, pause mid-stream, and let my defender jump thinking he was going to pack me. Once he flew past me, I would shoot a wide open 3 pointer! Swoosh! I love to watch NBA Players like Stephen Curry, Klay Thompson and former greats like Micahel Jordan, Reggie Miller and Larry Bird do this! This is what happens when you *Pause in His Presence*; the enemy flies past you and watches as you score the winning shot and lead someone to the Lord.

When I played football I learned sometimes in order to accelerate into the end zone and score a touchdown I couldn't always pound my way through my opponents. Sometimes I would have to pause or stutter-step and allow the defender to overrun me so I could waltz right into the endzone. I love watching NFL greats such as Jerry Rice and Emmit Smith. This is exactly what happens when you *Pause in His Presence*. The enemy overshoots you, then watches from behind as you breeze right into the endzone of the Harvest fields.

When I was a child I loved watching the Road Runner Cartoon. I especially liked it when he was being chased by the Wile E. Coyote. I would laugh every time when the Road Runner would simply pause outside of the path and let Wile E. Coyote keep running in circles. This is exactly what happens when you *Pause in His Presence.* The enemy will run in circles as you relax outside of his path drinking a glass of ice-tea!

Hit the Pause Button on the enemy!

"When everyone present heard those words, they erupted with furious rage. They mobbed Jesus and threw him out of the city, dragging him to the edge of the cliff on the hill on which the city had been built, ready to hurl him off. But he walked right through the crowd, leaving them all stunned."
Luke 4:28-30 (TPT)

Just like Jesus pressed the pause button and passed through the angry mob that wished to kill him, we too can press the pause button and pass right on through the plans of the enemy.

"The Heavenly Father does not ask for golden vessels. He does not ask for silver vessels. God asks for yielded vessels."
—*Kathryn Kuhlman*

Joshua Fowler with Zoë Fowler

Chapter 4

Presence + Nothing = Everything

"Some people wonder why they can't have faith for healing. They feed their body three hot meals a day, and their spirit one cold snack a week." — F. F. Bosworth

His presence plus nothing equals everything! Nothing else is needed to live a fulfilled life. Have you heard the statement, "Just add water"? Well, "Just add presence!" When the presence of God is added to your life, everything else will flow from the place of His presence. In His presence everything becomes more clear. Everything clicks. Everything works. Everything happens in His presence and nothing happens apart from His presence. Nothing else compares. The closest thing to it is the love of a spouse or your child or grandchild. But all of that is born through the presence of God. God is love so anything good was born in and through Him. We don't need another gimmick or add-on in our lives or church services. No! All we need is to learn to *Pause in His Presence.* We need to learn how to surrender in His love.

LEAN, LISTEN & LOVE

"God wants interdependence from us, not self-reliance. He puts us in a place of risk-taking so that we will connect to— and stay connected to—Him." — Shawn Bolz

Recently while *Pausing in His Presence* I heard the Lord say, "Lean, Listen & Love." There's a clarion call to "Lean into Jesus", lay your head upon His chest, listen to His heart, and love. As we do we will be caught up into deeper realms of His love and be able to express His love to others.

Lean

"Trust in the LORD with all your heart, And lean not on your own understanding;" Proverbs 3:5 (NKJV)

"Who out there fears GOD, actually listens to the voice of his servant? For anyone out there who doesn't know where you're going, anyone groping in the dark, Here's what: Trust in GOD. Lean on your God!" Isaiah 50:10 (MSG)

When I was growing up I loved to go to ball games and pep rallies! One of the songs we would sing while leaning back on each other was "Lean, lean, lean, lean lean, le-le-lean." Another song that I loved is, "Lean On Me, when you're not strong." I can still hear my grandparents church singing, "Leaning on the Everlasting Arms." The question is what are you leaning on? You can't lean on your own thoughts and feelings. You can't always lean on someone else. You have to lean fully on the Lord!

My daughter, Destiny, and her husband, Eben, are always having fun and out of the blue one of them will say, "trust-fall". Then they will fall back expecting the other one to catch them! If you lean into Heaven you will hear the Father say, "Trust fall!" He will catch you every time as you lean on Him and *Pause in His Presence.*

When I swam with my children when they were younger, I would say, "Jump , I've got you!" So it is with your Abba Father! Can you hear Him calling you, "Jump into the River of My Presence, I've got you."

"The disciple that Jesus dearly loved was at the right of him at the table and was leaning his head on Jesus." John 13:23 (TPT)

I heard the Lord say, "Tell My people to throw away the 'Crutches of Reasoning'. For reason is the reason you aren't seeing more of me. Reason is the reason you don't see more power. Reason is the reason you don't see more signs and wonders. Reason is the reason you don't see more healings and miracles. Reason is the reason you don't see more breakthroughs. Reason is the reason you aren't seeing more souls saved. Reason is the reason for the lack of harvest. Reason is the reason you don't see more of My glory. Reason is the reason you don't see more favor. Reason is the reason you don't have more finances. Reason is the reason you aren't having more prayers answered. Reason is the reason you're not receiving your dreams and desires. Reason is the reason you don't see more fulfillment. For too often you allow your reason to get in the way of what I have said and desire to do in your life. Too often you reason away the reason I came. You say, 'What if this and what if that?' You reason away what Holy Spirit is saying with worldly wisdom. Now is the time for you to lay down your own reasoning. You must stop leaning on your own understanding and trust in the Lord."

Listen

"Whoever will listen will hear the speaking Heaven." —A. W. Tozer

"Oh, that My people would listen to Me, That Israel would walk in My ways!" Psalms 81:13 (NKJV)

"Are your ears awake? Listen. Listen to the Wind Words, the Spirit blowing through the churches." Revelations 3:13 (MSG)

One of our greatest expressions of love unto the Lord and unto others is how intently we listen when they speak. Do we lock eyes with them? Humility is to place value on what someone else is saying. This means we listen without immediately forming a response. There are innumerable treasures waiting to be found in God's written word (logos) and spoken word (rhema). The only way we can unpack them is by listening, reading, and waiting without interrupting. God is always speaking to our hearts. There are waves in the spirit cascading throughout the day and when we stop to listen we will hear the sound of His love for His people. When we humble ourselves, turn our ears to the Lord, and wait on Him, we will capture what He is saying.

"Even when I cannot see him, I can hear the beautiful gallop of God's heartbeat for humanity." — *Christine Caine*

Do we have ears to hear? A prayer I have often prayed is, "Holy Spirit, teach me to seek God." The Spirit of God is continually searching the depths of God. (1 Corinthians 2:10) The Holy Spirit can teach you to *lean in* and *listen*! Many of us step foot into our spiritual scavenger hunts seeking things we want to find on *our* list. But today is the day to toss out the list and allow the Lord to reveal to us His mysteries, and through communion unveil deeper revelations in the secret place. God is inviting us, "Come away with Me! I have mysteries. I have things I want you to see! Come with child-like faith and wonder. Let's explore together!"

My dad, Dr. Charlie Fowler, told me a story once that went something like this: Years ago, a blackout occurred in a major city. All of the engineers could not get the power to come back on! It was a total blackout. Somebody remembered an old man who lived far out in the country. He came driving up in his old, rattling, beat and banged pick-up truck, pulled his old tattered tool box from the bed of the truck and limped in. He looked at the generator, and walked around a few times. After a little while he pulled out a small hammer, and walked around a couple more times. Then he tapped on the generator with the hammer. TAP! TAP! Immediately every single light in town came back on. People began to scream, cheer, holler and clap. The man walked over to his toolbox, put the hammer back in his toolbox and walked over to his beat up truck. Somebody said, "Hey, hey! Sir, how much do we owe ya?!" He replied, "Well, I reckon that will be around two thousand dollars." They said, "Two thousand dollars for two little taps?!" He said, "Nah, only a couple dollars for the taps. The rest is for knowing where to tap."

Many are leaning in and aimlessly tapping without listening for the Holy Spirit to teach them where to tap. The lie is that it takes: a large hammer, a degree, fancy lights, or a certain number of people in the room to somehow attain glory or a presence. The truth is that the key to entering into greater glory is intimacy and history. When you intimately know the Lord, with one TAP or two taps; you will glide into His presence and His glory will shine on you and your entire city. With one TAP you will hear the sound of His voice. With one note, you will TAP into glory. With one TAP, your city is saved. How? By leaning in, listening, and *pausing in His presence.*

Love

> *"Love from the center of who you are; don't fake it. Run for dear life from evil; hold on for dear life to good." Romans 12:9 (MSG)*
> *"The religious scholar answered, 'It states, "You must love the Lord God with all your heart, all your passion, all your energy, and your every thought. And you must love your neighbor as well as you love yourself."' Luke 10:27 (TPT)*

God is love! As we *Selah*, love will swell within our hearts and pour out of us like a waterfall. The enemy of this flow of love is: unforgiveness, anger, and hatred. I have seen in my life the freedom that comes through sacrificial love. I have experienced deep pain from people I trusted most. I have experienced deep pain from people I entrusted my heart with. However, when I chose to partake in the suffering of Jesus and receive His grace at work within me to forgive, I experienced radical encounters with the Lord.

Jesus was beaten, spit on, mocked, yelled at, accused, hated, and His response us the greatest display of sacrificial love we have ever seen. As these words flowed off of Jesus' lips to the ears of God, "Father, forgive them for they know not what they do."

Wow. This is sacrificial love. This is radical forgiveness. This is our example. When we realize how one we are with Jesus, we realize that offense has been absolutely destroyed. It is impossible to be offended or to harbor unforgiveness in our hearts, when we truly abide in union with Jesus. John 15 says to "abide in love." Jesus is the beautiful vine and we are the branches; branches of His love, forgiveness, life, peace, and joy in the earth. Let's extend ourselves further in love to everyone around us. I encourage you to lean into the Father, listen to His voice, and love on Him and others.

The Triple-H Principle

1. Hunger

"Blessed are those who hunger and thirst for righteousness, For they shall be filled." Matthew 5:6 (NKJV)

How hungry are you? Are you desperate for more of His presence in your life? Do you have yearnings and hunger pains for more of the Lord? Or are you satisfied with a little dab on a Sunday morning? Are you present in His presence? Or do you find your life consumed by entertainment? In a day and hour where everything is tugging and vying for our attention we must become more intentional in our pursuit of His presence.

Most of the world has a constant distraction that has become another appendage to our bodies. It seems many can't do anything without it. It draws us every hour of the day. It doesn't wait for normal business hours. It's pushy. It's bossy. It's overwhelming. It's addictive. Both adults and children alike cannot seem to get enough of it. We seem to be glued to it at all hours of the day. The very thing that was meant to bring people together and provide avenues of communication, in many cases has done the exact opposite. It has divided, isolated and taken over our every waking moment. It's hard to believe that something so small has become so big in the lives of so many. In most cases it's something that can fit in the palm of your hand. It seems to rule our world. Isn't it amazing that something less than 6' inches long and 3' inches wide can be so intrusive? This object has come between marriages and divided parents from children. Yep, you guessed it, it's your smartphone. In some cases it could be called the opposite, a dumb phone!

Apostle Paul admonished that most things are okay when done in moderation. However, it appears most of mankind struggles with overcoming obsessive, compulsive and addictive behaviors. Whether it's a: smartphone addiction, overeating, exercising, gaming, shopping, golfing, gambling, drugs or other forms of entertainment, it seems as if our nature is to become excessive at best and addicts at worse. Too often our inability to set boundaries allows the very things that were designed for our pleasure, to become our slave-masters! Imagine this same nature, but toward God's presence. May we be consumed with longings, cravings, and hunger for more His presence.

"When we pursue kingdom principles above His presence, we are looking for the kingdom without a king." —Bill Johnson

When you're hungry you set down your phone to pick up a fork. So it is with whatever is between you and more of His presence. If you are truly hungry for more of the Lord, you'll set aside anything that's getting in the way of you being filled with more of His presence. Jesus is the Bread of Life. John 6:27 says, "Do not work for the food that perishes, but for the food that endures to eternal life, which the Son of Man will give to you. For on him God the Father has set his seal."

Create space for Jesus. Make room for Him. In the morning, let the first words off of your lips be praise. During work or responsibilities, anchor yourself in His nearness. Just as you can run to social media in a split second, run to Him. Fill yourself with Jesus! If you eat too much junk food, you can't fuel up on that which is truly good for you. You only have so much bandwidth. Ask the Holy Spirit, "What is in my life that is encroaching on Jesus's place in my life? Make me jealous for Your presence. Help me to guard my secret place."

Hunger
By: David & Nicole Binion (Feat. MDSN)

There's a hunger and a thirst
I'm desperate, immerse me
I'm not waiting anymore
I need you, Lord
I need you, Lord

As people of hunger, we must give His presence preference. We must give Him preferential treatment. Jesus should have first dibs on us, our time, and our lives. The children of Israel set up camp around the tabernacle. They moved when He said to move and camped when He said

69

to camp. They followed the Cloud by Day and the Fire by night. We are called to plan our days around His presence!

2. Humility

"and My people, who are called by My Name, humble themselves, and pray and seek (crave, require as a necessity) My face and turn from their wicked ways, then I will hear [them] from heaven, and forgive their sin and heal their land." 2 Chronicles 7:14 (AMP)

"But He gives more grace. Therefore He says: 'God resists the proud, But gives grace to the humble.'" James 4:6 (NKJV)

"Likewise, you younger men [of lesser rank and experience], be subject to your elders [seek their counsel]; and all of you, clothe yourselves with humility toward one another [tie on the servant's apron], for God is opposed to the proud [the disdainful, the presumptuous, and He defeats them], but He gives grace to the humble." 1 Peter 5:5 (AMP)

How Low Can You Go?

One of the Hebrew words for worship is, "shachah" - sounds like we are praying in tongues! "Shachah" means to bow down, or to prostrate oneself. When I "shacah," I get into position to receive more of His presence. If I want a download, I have to get down low. When I humble myself, He will exalt me. Exalt means, "to lift or elevate to a higher place." We are invited to take a seat next to Him in Heavenly places! (Eph. 2:6)

The Kiss of Reverence!

One of the Greek words for worship "proskuneo" means "to kiss the hand towards one in token of reverence." It means " to kneel or prostrate to pay homage." When I kneel and I bow down, I am positioned to kiss the hand of God. When one goes before the King, they always bow. In Asia, the culture is humility. In fact, the culture is always to be lower than the one who is in authority. That's the way it is supposed to work, but many have lost this culture of honor in America. People are going to do what they want to do, when they want to do it, and no one is going to be over them. Many have become lawless and rebellious, and it's robbing them of more of God's presence. If you cannot bow before the Lord or submit to His word, and His delegated authority in your life, then you will not experience more of His presence.

Many have lost the ability to get low in the church. You know why so many people are getting their heads cut off in the war? Why so many people are getting blown to bits in this war that we are in for the Kingdom? It is because we have our head up in pride! When men are in war they have to stay low, moving in unity and in submission to authority. They don't run around asking to be hit or shot. Men in war move carefully with a great awareness to the bullets flying, stay low, and focus on the mission at hand.

A Title or a Towel?

Why do we have to get low? It's in wisdom so we don't get hit by a fiery dart of the enemy! We have too many believers and leaders, with heads lifted high, and this is absolutely contrary to the nature and character of Christ. In fact, Jesus bent down on His knees and washed His disciples feet. The question I am asking you today is simple. Are you looking for a title or a towel? Are you willing to humble yourself and wash the feet of the next generation?

The Oil Flows Down!

To live in God's glory and blessing, you have to live a life that is submitted to authority. Many people don't like that word, "submit." But it is impossible to move forward if you don't come under authority. You can't upgrade if you're not under authority. Submission simply means, "I'm coming under the mission." Everything we do must come into alignment with that. If it does not come in alignment with our mission, I submit. Like a sub in the water, I go under and I come under that mission.

That is how I am blessed according to Psalms 133:1, " Behold how good and how pleasant it is for brethren to dwell together in unity. It is like the oil that ran down Aaron's beard even unto his garments." You can't get the oil unless you become a part of the garments of the house. "It's like the dew upon the mountains." You have to be on that mountain to receive the dew that comes from the top down. When snow hits the mountain, where does it hit first? The top, and it comes down. It releases the flow for anyone that is on that mountain. The streams that flow through that mountain are replenished from the Heavens. Why? Because the oil flows down. The oil gathers in the hems of the garment. If you'll humble yourself the oil will increase in your life. As they touch those who are a part of the hem, they will touch Him!

From The Basement to The Penthouse!

If you're dreaming of living in the penthouse, you have to learn how to first live in the basement. The Bible says, "He that abases himself, he that humbles himself, I will exalt. But he who exalts himself, I will abase." The way up is down. Lift your hands in worship! It even looks like a pause sign as you lift your hands. "Lift your paws!" (Haha!) I pray that every time you raise your hands it will be a reminder to pause in His presence.

3. Honor

"Honor empowers people." —Danny Silk

In the Jewish culture, when the oldest son comes of age, everything that the parents had was bestowed upon that child. When everything is bestowed upon that child, you know what happens? His parents become his responsibility. He says, you provided covering for me, so now I will take care of you. Now, that is honor! There have been seasons where I have watched my dad take care of his dad and mom. He gave them food, paid their car payment and house payment; he took care of them. You know why? Because they took care of him when he had nothing! They raised him and honored him, and he did it in return. Blessing flows in honor!

Who are we to honor?

1. *God*
2. *His Word*
3. *His Delegated Authority*
4. *One Another*

How do we increase our ability to carry God's Presence?

Anything you are thankful for increases. Live your life every day releasing expressions of a thankful heart, and you will see God's presence increase. Gratefulness enlarges our capacity for more of Him! The Greek translation of 1 Corinthians 14 reveals *only* one place where we are allowed to have a lustful pursuit of something, and that's for His presence!

You can't have something you're unwilling to bestow honor in the life of someone else! Don't compare yourself with others. Don't degrade what you have. Be thankful for the measure you have and you will receive more. Steward the measure you have received, and you will receive more. Honor the measure that you've been given, and it will increase more and more!

"Honor is the hover lane of heaven. You can't drive on it alone. You have to honor someone and help them along in order to accelerate into your destiny, too!" — Joshua Fowler

Have you ever noticed when you are looking for something or you buy something new that you see it more and more. Perhaps you desire a certain car or color of a new shirt and then suddenly everywhere you look you see it. The more you become aware of God the more you will see Him, and the more you will reveal Him to others. What you look for, you will see! Seek and you will find. Awareness produces readiness! Your awareness of God's presence attracts more of His presence!

Doxa, is a Greek word for worship: meaning the opinion, the estimate, whether good or bad concerning someone. It goes on to mean: the opinion concerning one, resulting in praise, honor, glory, splendor, brightness, excellence, preeminence, dignity, grace and majesty. It is a thing belonging to God. Doxa! That worship is an appraisal of God. How much do you estimate God to be worth? What is your estimation of Him, and His glory? What is your appraisal of God?

Honor = Value / Appraisal

Not long ago, we had an accident. An insurance appraiser was sent to evaluate the damage to the car. After the damage inspection, the company sent a check to repair the damages. They had to first estimate and appraise the value of the damage. When I buy a house, that appraisal of the house gives me the ability to present the bank with information that will get a loan to purchase the house. The appraisal qualifies what I should spend on it, or if I want to buy it with cash. If I want to buy my next house with cash, I don't want to pay over the appraised value. If I'm wise, I will even try to get it for less than the appraisal.

We have people whose appraisal of God is coming in way too low. Their *doxa* of God is too low. We have to get to a place where our appraisal of God is praiseworthy! Our appraisal of God should be remarkably high! We should esteem Him so high that we are willing to stay low and willing to dance and praise. We need to give God the worship that He is due! He is worthy of full abandonment and sacrifice.

God is everything and we are nothing without Him. Let's bow before Him! If praise comes from a mindset that we are doing God a favor, or if it is more about self than it is about Him, then we are missing out on the upload. Our worship needs to be a lavish offering to the One who gave it all! No more lip service! It is time to shift from speaking and singing "things", but with hearts that are far from Him. There is a place of authentic, wholehearted, genuine expression that we abide in when we truly honor God and His presence.

Don't you hate it when someone turns the internet signal off suddenly? When that happens, you lose what you were doing. Don't you think God hates it, too? You are uploading, and all the sudden, there is a disconnect! That's the way God feels. We start to worship Him, but then we get a text. We're worshiping Him, but then the phone rings. We're worshiping Him, but then we "need" to look at social media. We are distracted in our worship, instead of being Davidic in our worship!

Dishonor delays destiny, but honor accelerates destiny!

Your appraisal of God is a reverse appraisal. It appraises you! If my appraisal of God is low, my appraisal of His house is low. My value of being at His house will be low because my appraisal of God is low. Now, my appraisal of God becomes a reverse appraisal of my own life, because my self-worth comes from His self-worth. If I don't value Him, I won't value me after a while. If I don't put the right value on my covenant with God, then I won't value my marriage. That appraisal flows from this relationship into every relationship I have.

I want to *doxa* God. I want to give an appraisal of God, the best appraisal that I can come up with. In fact, if I praise Him to the best of my ability, it would not be enough, but how incredible is it that He loves the offering of our lives! The Lord placed an image of myself as a little child offering Him my heart. With a big smile I looked up into His kind eyes and said, "Here, Abba! Here's my heart!" Overjoyed at my gift, He smiled, and He took my heart into His hands. He said, "My child, I love your heart so much. I will heal every wound, clean up all the dirt, and make all things new!" God is worthy of our hearts; worthy of our all. When we *doxa* God, it isn't from a place of perfection, but it is an extravagant response to our recognition of His surpassing worth.

"After this I looked, and, behold, a door was opened in heaven: and the first voice which I heard was as it were of a trumpet talking with me; which said, Come up hither, and I will shew thee things which must be hereafter. And immediately I was in the spirit: and, behold, a throne was set in heaven, and one sat on the throne. And

he that sat was to look upon like a jasper and a sardine stone: and there was a rainbow round about the throne, in sight like unto an emerald. And round about the throne were four and twenty seats: and upon the seats I saw four and twenty elders sitting, clothed in white raiment; and they had on their heads crowns of gold. And out of the throne proceeded lightnings and thunderings and voices: and there were seven lamps of fire burning before the throne, which are the seven Spirits of God. And before the throne there was a sea of glass like unto crystal: and in the midst of the throne, and round about the throne, were four beasts full of eyes before and behind. And the first beast was like a lion, and the second beast-like a calf, and the third beast had a face as a man, and the fourth beast was like a flying eagle. And the four beasts had each of them six wings about him; and they were full of eyes within: and they rested not day and night, saying, Holy, holy, holy, Lord God Almighty, which was, and is, and is to come. And when those beasts give glory and honor and thanks to him that sat on the throne, who liveth for ever and ever, The four and twenty elders fall down before him that sat on the throne, and worship him that liveth for ever and ever, and cast their crowns before the throne, saying, Thou art worthy, O Lord, to receive glory and honor and power: for thou hast created all things, and for thy pleasure they are and were created."
Revelations 4 (KJV)

We can see Heaven through John's eyes and get a glimpse of what Heaven is like. When the Lord encountered me as a sixteen-year-old boy in Wisconsin. He opened up Heaven, and I hit my knees. I heard Heaven; I heard worship like I have never heard before. I heard the sounds of His presence. He said, "Worship Me! It is the closest place on earth to Me. Teach My people to worship Me!" From that place of worship, from that place of intimacy, I have tried to live my life. This passage gives us a glimpse of that, and God shows what is happening around the throne. On earth as it is in heaven!

In Revelation 5, we see that worship is due unto Lion of the Tribe of Judah. The last verse of chapter 4 says, "for thou hast created all things, and for thy pleasure they are and were created." You must remember this statement: "I was created for His pleasure." Realize that you were created for God's pleasure. You have been created to make His praise glorious! When you realize that you were created for God's pleasure you will experience the overflow of heaven.

In John 10:10, Jesus said, "I come that you might have life and that you might have life more abundantly." The Amplified Version says "filled to the full, to the overflow." The overflow life where you walk with such glory that it is squishing and leaking even from your shoes. You are called to permeate with His presence. You should be releasing His fragrance everywhere you go. Why? Because when the evaporation of the proper evaluation of God in worship (honor!) goes up, His presence will pour back down in rain.

Then you will be able to say, "What do you need? Healing? Get close to me because I have been spending time with the Healer! Do you need a breakthrough in your finances? Spend time with me, because I have been spending time with the God who owns it all. Do you need favor? I have been rubbing shoulders with the King of Kings; I have been laying my head on His chest and loving on Him. I just happen to know somebody that can do something for you!" It doesn't come from here on earth; it comes from spending time with Him. "Seek first the Kingdom of God and His righteousness, and all these things will be added to you!"

Honor Scriptures:

"That's where he restores and revives my life. He opens before me pathways to God's pleasure and leads me along in his footsteps of righteousness so that I can bring honor to his name."
Psalms 23:3 (TPT)

"Be in awe before his majesty. Be in awe before such power and might! Come worship wonderful Yahweh, arrayed in all his splendor, bowing in worship as he appears in the beauty of

holiness. Give him the honor due his name. Worship him wearing the glory-garments of your holy, priestly calling!"
Psalms 29:2 (TPT)

"For the commandment, 'Honor your father and your mother,' was the first of the Ten Commandments with a promise attached:"
Ephesians 6:2 (TPT)

"Lord, how wonderful you are! You have stored up so many good things for us, like a treasure chest heaped up and spilling over with blessings— all for those who honor and worship you! Everybody knows what you can do for those who turn and hide themselves in you." Psalms 31:9 (TPT)

"Honor me by trusting in me in your day of trouble. Cry aloud to me, and I will be there to rescue you." Psalms 50:15 (TPT)

"And the blessings keep coming! Then all the ends of the earth will give him the honor he deserves and be in awe of him!"
Psalms 67:7 (TPT)

"Teach me more about you, how you work and how you move, so that I can walk onward in your truth until everything within me brings honor to your name." Psalms 86:11 (TPT)

"Never stingy and always generous to those in need, their lives of influence and honor will never be forgotten, for they were full of good deeds." Psalms 112:9 (TPT)

"Be devoted to tenderly loving your fellow believers as members of one family. Try to outdo yourselves in respect and honor of one another." Romans 12:10 (TPT)

Pause In His Presence

It's time for a Selah Session!

Take a few moments and ask the Holy Spirit to cultivate within you a lifestyle of Hunger, Humility, and Honor!

Selah Scriptures:

_____

_____

_____

_____

_____

_____

Pause Prayers:

_____

_____

_____

_____

_____

_____

_____

_____

Pause Promises & Prophecies:

_____

_____

_____

_____

_____

_____

_____

Selah Reflections:

_____

_____

_____

_____

_____

_____

_____

_____

_____

Chapter 5

Enemies of The Pause

"An enemy is someone who increases, strengthens, encourages, or enables an area of weakness in you that God wants to remove from your life."— Ron Carpenter

You were created to be a person of God's presence! There are several things that try to distract us from living in His presence which I will address in this chapter. It's crucial to identify these things so that we can abide in passionate, first-love pursuit. Living as a *Presence Carrier* flows through the currency of purity, so we have to guard our hearts from anything that might try to steal the throne of our hearts. We must guard our hearts from "*foxes that try to spoil the garden*". (Song of Solomon 2:15)

- **Pleasure**
- **Prosperity**
- **Performance**
- **Programs**

Pleasure or Presence?

"Turn my eyes from worthless things, and give me life through your word." Psalm 119:37 (NLT)

Today is the day to forsake the lifestyle of comfortable and convenient Christianity! If you want the oil of His presence, you can't live life from pleasure to pleasure. The pleasures of this world are seasonal with a speedily approaching expiration date. However, God's presence will sustain you, uphold you, and revive you! It's alright to enjoy nice things and to walk in favor and blessings. Just don't allow your first pursuit to become pleasures. If we aren't careful we will miss out on more of Him by substituting resting in His presence with a night of entertainment or a weekend away. Time is our most precious commodity! How we spend it determines what we value and what increases in our lives. Let's value His presence and become more and more aware of Him every day.

Prosperity or Presence?

"The fear of the Lord is clean, enduring forever; The judgments of the Lord are true and righteous altogether. More to be desired are they than gold, Yea, than much fine gold; Sweeter also than honey and the honeycomb. Moreover by them Your servant is warned. And in keeping them there is great reward." Psalm 19:9-11 (NKJV)

One day as I was in prayer the Lord said to me, "Wealth is in your worship and gold is in my glory." We're not called to set our eyes on riches and wealth, but on His presence! Posture yourself in worship. More blessed is it to give. Pour yourself out as a liquid offering. As you pour yourself out at the feet of Jesus, you will experience the wealth and glory that overflows in His presence alone. When we pursue His presence we will prosper in every area of our lives.

Performance or Presence?

"Royalty is my identity. Servanthood is my assignment. Intimacy with God is my life source."—Bill Johnson

Humility, teachability, and brokenness are what will counteract and break the performance mentality. Excellence is wonderful, but when it's at the expense of the raw, true Gospel, it is not from the heart of God. No longer can we settle for church without God's presence. My heart has been broken to see auditoriums watered down to fog, light shows, and nice Readers Digest sermons, but at the end His presence wasn't ever there.

There are eyes fastened on celebrity preachers, but many have learned how to do it without anointing, and without oil. Many know exactly when to put their hand up here. They know when to wait for the applause, and how to move people's emotions. But God doesn't want a show. God wants lives drenched in His presence and saturated with His glory to the point that when we speak it doesn't come from emotions, but from the presence of the living God.

This oil flows from the throne. It flows from the midst of His presence. This oil isn't found in a set list, performance, or hype. This oil is found in radical pursuit of His presence. This oil is found seeking His face. This oil is found in utter dependency on the presence of the Lord.

Programs or Presence?

"Don't try and fit your faith into your busy schedule, build your schedule around your faith." — Kenneth Copeland

All too often churches have replaced presence with programs. Sometimes this is the result of trying to meet the demands of people and other times it happens because leaders are looking for shortcuts for church growth. This is true especially in the American church. Many have tried to bring over a fast-food mentality into the church. At best many are replacing homemade meals with Minute rice, instant potatoes and frozen meals. I'm all for systems. However, systems without His Spirit are powerless. We need systems that are submitted to the Holy Spirit!

"God doesn't act like the Church. No, instead, the Church must act like God." — Kim Clement

Herding people in and out of a building for a 55-85 minute experience will never take the place of a true encounter with the presence of the Lord. We are being told by "growth church experts" that the optimal time of worship is 13 minutes and the message needs to be 28 minutes or less. These same experts say we shouldn't talk about the offering and let people give if they want at the door on the way out of the building. They tell us we shouldn't allow any expressions of the gifts of the Holy Spirit in our services, and if we do that we should relegate it to a special service once a month or to home groups. God's House is no longer His House. We treat Him as if He were a guest and we are the master of the house.

Awkwardly Awaiting The Master of The House!

Have you ever visited someone's home to find that they weren't home? Perhaps their children offered you some coffee or tea as you felt awkward and awaited their arrival. This is the case in many churches today. People visit and the Master of the house isn't home; nor is He welcome. Then some churches treat God like He's their Jack-in-the-box and they wind Him up and say, "God's Here!" only to push him back in their box when they're ready to move on to something else.

Lord, we repent! Bring us back to a pure pursuit. Bring us back to the simplicity of presence. Bring us back to our first love. Remove every distraction and give us eyes that are fixated on You.

The Davidic Pattern ushers in The Presence of God!

God is a God of consistency. He is the same yesterday, today, and forever. Our hearts beat around 100,000 times a day in consistent patterns. The sun rises and sets on a consistent pattern. There are numerous patterns from the Old Testament that we can capture through the lens of Jesus and apply in our lives today. One of those patterns is found in the sixth chapter of second Samuel. Like many "Uzzah-friendly" churches are finding out today, David learned the hard way that you cannot bring the presence of God on a cart!

The "cart" can be described as humanity's way of thinking. The cart is in many churches today and comes hidden in the form of programs, good ideas, popularity contests, politics, and traditions of men. The death of Uzzah (2 Samuel 6:7), whose name means "strength," clearly reveals that we cannot harness, dictate, or control the move of God with our natural strength or abilities.

After Uzzah's death, King David sought the Lord for direction. In 2 Samuel 6:9, David was afraid of the LORD that day; and he said, "How can the ark of the LORD come to me?" Let this be a prayer that flows from our hearts to His. "Lord, how can I position myself to draw Your presence into my life?" This is the cry of a yielded son and daughter desperate to create an environment that will house the presence of God.

David sent his servants to search the Scriptures to see how to move the Ark. He discovered in the Word of God that the Ark (presence) of the Lord must be carried on the shoulders of the priests. The Word of God declares that once King David set things in order by having the priests carry the Ark and make sacrifices to God, he was able to lead all of Israel into the city in a procession of victorious praise. David danced before the Ark of the Lord with all his might, and the people shouted and played instruments. (1 Chron. 15:26-28.) When we *Pause in His Presence*, we surrender our way of doing things. When we seek God's way we will experience fullness of joy in His presence!

Once the Ark was safely brought back to Jerusalem, they set it in a tent that David had pitched specifically for it. Then David stationed Levites to minister before the Ark (presence) of the Lord, to *record*, to *thank*, and to *praise* the Lord God of Israel continually, 24/7, 365 days a year. (1 Chron. 16:1,4,37.) The tabernacle of David was a tent that housed the Ark (presence) of the Lord where four thousand musicians and 288 singers were stationed to minister to the Lord 24/7, 365 days a year, in intercession, praise, and worship (1 Chron. 23:5; 25:7).

Perhaps you are asking yourself, is this really for today? And if so, how can we rebuild it? Yes, it is for today! Starting with King David and his son Solomon, this pattern has been handed down as an eternal, heavenly pattern: *"And the pattern of all that he had by the spirit"* (1 Chron. 28:12 KJV). Not only is it for today, but it is a pattern that we can carry into every part of our lives.

In the secret place, we can seek God's face with words of insatiable hunger and selfless pursuit rushing off of our lips and into His heart. In our families, we can lift our voices together in worship, pour out our adoration, and lean in as He draws in to meet with us and to strengthen us as a family unit. In our churches, we can toss out the rigid formulas and agendas that are intended only to see a certain number of people filling the seats and instead prepare a throne of praise for King Jesus. In our businesses, we can forsake selfish ambition and proclaim that all of our finances are for Kingdom advancement.

"It came even to pass, as the trumpeters and singers were as one, to make one sound to be heard in praising and thanking the Lord; and when they lifted up their voice with the trumpets and cymbals and instruments of music, and praised the Lord, saying, For He is good; for His mercy endureth for ever: that then the house was filled with a cloud, even the house of the Lord; so that the priests could not stand to minister by reason of the cloud: for the glory of the Lord had filled the house of God." 2 Chronicles 5:13 (NKJV)

Every leader who followed the pattern that David received from the Lord possessed promises and prospered! The Word of God gives accounts of seven leaders who followed this pattern of the tabernacle of David. Two of these leaders were Nehemiah and Hezekiah. Nehemiah rebuilt the walls by building just David did. (Nehemiah 11 and 12.)

"And he [Hezekiah] did what was right in the sight of the Lord, according to all that his father David had done. In the first year of his reign, in the first month, he opened the doors of the house of the Lord and repaired them. Then he brought in the priests and the Levites, and gathered them in the East Square, and said to them: 'Hear me, Levites! Now sanctify yourselves, sanctify the house of the Lord God of your fathers, and carry out the rubbish from the holy place.'" 2 Chronicles 29:2-5 (NKJV)

The glory of the Lord will always fill a house that is built according to His Word and centered around Him! It is undeniable. The glory of the Lord is going to fill your house because you are surrendering yourself for God-encounters by pausing in His presence. Each pause, lean into the sound of His voice. Each pause, become more acquainted with His Word. Each pause, sync yourself more and more with His heart.

Let's continue diving into the Tabernacle of David. In Matthew 21:13 and Isaiah 56:7, Jesus and Isaiah called the tabernacle of David "the house of prayer." The Apostle John revealed the beauty of the tabernacle of David in Revelation 4 and 5. In Acts 13:2, we see the priestly principle of ministering to God as found in the tabernacle of David. In this passage, leaders ministered to God and, as a result, the Apostles Paul and Barnabas were sent forth to change the world. We find that once the Tabernacle of David was rebuilt, God's glory overtook cities and nations. As this happens in the Church today, we will reap the greatest harvest of souls that the world has ever known.

The Davidic pattern ushers in glory, harvest and God's presence.

The only way for us to rebuild the tabernacle of David is to create a habitation in which God can dwell. We do so through passionate, corporate praise and worship, and through united, fervent intercessory prayer. This requires pure, sincere hearts of men and women who will set their eyes on the Lord, and not on anything else.

His Presence Positions Us for Possession

"In that [this] day will I raise up the tabernacle of David that is fallen, and close up the breaches thereof; and I will raise up his ruins, and I will build it as in the days of old: That they may possess the remnant of Edom, and of all the heathen, which are called by My name, saith the Lord that doeth this. Behold, the days come, saith the Lord, that the plowman shall overtake the reaper, and the treader of grapes him that soweth seed;and the mountains shall drop sweet wine,and all the hills shall melt. And I will bring again the captivity of My people of Israel, and they shall build the waste cities, and inhabit them; and they shall plant vineyards, and drink the wine thereof; they shall also make gardens, and eat the fruit of them. And I will plant them upon their land, and they shall no more be pulled up out of their land which I have given them, saith the Lord thy God." Amos 9:11-15 (NKJV)

5 Blessings of Rebuilding the Tabernacle of David

1. We will Possess the Harvest! (souls, souls, souls)

2. We will Possess New Wine! (refreshing, renewal, and revival)

3. We will Possess, Rebuild, and Inhabit Cities!

4. We will Possess Provision! (and the devil can't steal it)

5. We will Possess the Land! (forever, never to be evicted)

Are you ready to possess the harvest? Are you thirsty for the new wine of the Holy Spirit? Are you passionate about transforming your city? Does living in the land of more than enough sound good? Are you tired of being a "wilderness walker"? If so, trade your sandals in for mountain boots and arise as a "promise possessor". Now is the time to arise with a Davidic anointing as Nehemiah and Hezekiah did, wielding the sword of praise with one hand and the trowel of prayer with the other hand. Together we will rebuild the walls of the Tabernacle of David and possess the land through the presence of God!

Rebuilding the tabernacle of David is not just for the corporate Body of Christ; it is for you personally, as you walk through your life and ministry! Allow this pattern of the tabernacle of David to take root in your family and in your house. Center your life around His presence. Center your family around pursuit!

Pause In His Presence

It's time for a Selah Session!

Take some time and ask the Lord to reveal to you anywhere performance, pleasure, programs, or prosperity have tried to take precedence over His presence. When His presence has the first place, you will be positioned for possession!

Selah Scriptures:

_____

_____

_____

_____

_____

Pause Prayers:

_____

_____

_____

_____

_____

_____

Pause Promises & Prophecies:

_____

_____

_____

_____

_____

_____

_____

Selah Reflections:

_____

_____

_____

_____

_____

_____

_____

_____

Chapter 6

The P.A.U.S.E. Principle

"Will we be content to rest in our pew or kneel in His rest? There is glory awaiting us at the feet of God." —Bishop Joseph Garlington

Presence Centered

When the Children of Israel set up camp the Ark of the Covenant was always in the center. Everything revolved around the presence of God. This is how we must live our lives and gather in worship. Not around a personality, program, or people but Centered around His presence.

What is your life centered around? In the morning when you wake up, what is your first thought? How do you schedule your day, week, month, year? Many look at seeking the Lord as something on the top of the to-do-list. It sounds right, doesn't it? Instead of seeing God's Presence as another item on a list, see it as the center, the core, the very middle of who you are; the very purpose you were created.

Live from Him, in Him, and unto Him.
Abide from His love; from His affirmation.
Run your race from victory, not for victory.
He's inviting you today, "My child,
Pause in My Presence. Stay awhile."

In 2016, I began writing a song in my prayer closet, *Stay Awhile*, which we released under Legacy Worship. My daughter came to the keyboard with me in Canton, Ohio at around 2 in the morning to worship and finish the song. The words just flowed from my heart, inviting the Lord to stay awhile. A visitation won't do. My heart is longing for a habitation! When you first open your eyes in the morning, do you look into His eyes? When you go to get your morning coffee, do you bump into Jesus? When room is made for Him, and He is invited, He will come.

Stay Awhile
By: Joshua Fowler and Zoë Fowler

Come on in, You are welcome here.
Come on in, and stay awhile.
Come on in, You are my desire.
Come on in, and stay awhile.

Make this house Your home.
Make our lives Your own.
Make our hearts Your throne.
You're all that really matters!

Stay awhile! Stay awhile! Stay awhile!

When we recorded the song in 2017, the Lord swept into the room and responded to us. Our Father sang these words back to us!

"Come on in, You are welcome here!
Come on in, and stay awhile!
Come on in, You are My beloved child.
Come on in, and stay awhile!

Won't you climb up in my lap, and lay your head upon My chest child, just to see how much daddy loves you. Daddy loves you!"

You are a beloved child of God. He loves you with an outrageous, everlasting, immeasurable love. As you invite Him to stay awhile, He invites you to stay awhile. You were designed to abide in the place of His presence. You were made to stay awhile.

Pause In His Presence

It's time for a Selah Session!

The Father is whispering to your heart, "My beloved child, stay awhile."

Selah Scriptures:

_____

_____

_____

_____

_____

Pause Prayers:

_____

_____

_____

_____

_____

_____

_____

Pause Promises & Prophecies:

_____

_____

_____

_____

_____

_____

_____

Selah Reflections:

_____

_____

_____

_____

_____

_____

_____

_____

_____

Abandon Agendas

Have you ever went to see someone and they've had the whole day planned out so much so that you don't even have a spare moment to have a normal conversation? Or have you ever gone to a theme park with someone that should've been a drill sergeant instead of a guide? This is the way the Holy Spirit must feel in a lot of our lives and church services. This is how many people treat Him:

"Come here, Holy Spirit."
"Move here Holy Spirit."
"Not now, Holy Spirit."
"Wait until the next stop, Holy Spirit."
"Stay Here, Holy Spirit."
"Speak now, Holy Spirit."
"No, Holy Spirit, that is not on our agenda."
"Not here, Holy Spirit, that might offend someone."

I think you get the point. Often, we have everything so timed and planned out that there's no room for the Holy Spirit to take us where He wants to take us. This is how relationships become stale and cold. This is how churches become stale and cold!

In order to live in the overflow of His presence, we must abandon our agendas and allow the Holy Spirit to take the lead in our lives and church services again. In a wedding dance the groom leads and the bride follows. We must realize our place is to yield, follow and trust. Even as leaders, we must learn to pause and wait on the Groom to lead us in His Divine Dance.

Undivided & Unleashed Passion

With undivided hearts and unleashed passion we must pursue the Lover of our souls. We must step out into the mystery, and go beyond, further than we've ever been. There is so much more! Undivided devotion and unleashed passion is what it will take to get there.

Like David, let's go beyond in worship and become more undignified in praise!

Like Jacob, let's go beyond with the tenacity of a bull-dog, holding on until The Lord unveils true identity and destiny.

Like the woman with the issue of blood, let's go beyond in our faith and press in until we are healed and whole.

Strike The Ground

"And he said, 'Open the east window'; and he opened it. Then Elisha said, 'Shoot'; and he shot. And he said, 'The arrow of the Lord's deliverance and the arrow of deliverance from Syria; for you must strike the Syrians at Aphek till you have destroyed them.' Then he said, 'Take the arrows'; so he took them. And he said to the king of Israel, 'Strike the ground'; so he struck three times, and stopped. And the man of God was angry with him, and said, 'You should have struck five or six times; then you would have struck Syria till you had destroyed it! But now you will strike Syria only three times.'" 2 Kings 13:17-19 (NKJV)

When Elisha told the King to take a bow and arrow and shoot an arrow out the east window, he was showing us through a prophetic act how to look beyond where we are and defeat the enemy. Then, when Elisha told him to take the arrows and strike the ground, he was showing us how to live a life of lasting breakthrough and victory through unleashed passion.

We can't do this with a halfway, part-time, limp-noodle, milk-toast, week-knee, in today and out tomorrow attitude. NO! We must rise up with every fiber of our being! We must go all out with the pedal to the metal until we cross the finish line beneath the checkered flag of more of Him. We must have the pursuit of an uncaged lion for his prey. We must leave it all on the field. Not one drop of energy or sweat left inside of us or wasted on the sideline of the opinions of men. It will take everything we've got poured out in unleashed passion for more of Him.

"Revival isn't cheap! Revival isn't a basement bargain. Revival never goes on sale, it will cost you everything!" —Joshua Fowler

"So Jesus answered and said to them, 'Have faith in God. For assuredly, I say to you, whoever says to this mountain, "Be removed and be cast into the sea," and does not doubt in his heart, but believes that those things he says will be done, he will have whatever he says. Therefore I say to you, whatever things you ask when you pray, believe that you receive them, and you will have them.'" Mark 11:22-24 (NKJV)

Have you ever attended a fire-filled, Pentecostal church service where the congregation responds to the minister as he preaches? I grew up in a church like this! It's so much fun! Sometimes someone will play the Hammond B3 Organ and the people will shout aloud. There was dancing in the aisles. I can still hear some of those saints say, "Amen! Say it Pastor!" Well, if you stop and listen I believe you will hear the host of heaven cheering you on saying, "Say it Son! Say it Daughter!"

Heaven is empowered by your words. Are your words empowering light or darkness? Are your words advancing the kingdom of Heaven or Hell? Are your words pronouncing death or life? Are your words distancing you from Jesus or drawing Him in closer?

"Saying what the Father is saying releases the creative nature and presence of God into a situation to bring His influence and change." — *Bill Johnson*

Pause In His Presence

It's time for a Selah Session!

Take a moment with the Holy Spirit and dedicate your words to the Lord. Ask Him to teach you how to speak to your kids, spouse, friends, co-workers, and enemies, the way He wants you to. Declare it. "My words are for Your glory. My words are for your Kingdom. My words speak life."

Selah Scriptures:

_____

_____

_____

_____

_____

_____

Pause Prayers:

_____

_____

_____

_____

_____

_____

Pause Promises & Prophecies:

_____

_____

_____

_____

_____

_____

_____

Selah Reflections:

_____

_____

_____

_____

_____

_____

_____

_____

Decree it!

In the middle of the pause, God is going to help you recognize the authority you have in Him. Right in the middle is the time to press into His presence and partner with His word. His name and His Word are exalted above everything! As God's acting agents here on earth, you have the power to make decisions and decrees that will alter the course of history. You are a history maker. You are a world changer. You are a nation shaker. God sent you here for such a time as this. Your words matter! What you say and what you do has the power of death and life in it. If you decree a thing it shall be established.

Decree (noun): a formal and authoritative order, especially one having the force of law.

Decree (verb): to command or ordain, to decide by decree; a judicial decision or order.

The first mention of the word, decree, hermetically & etymologically speaking, is found in Job 22:28. The Hebrew word for "decree" is *gä-zar*, which means to cut, divide, cut down, split and destroy.

"Thou also shall decree a thing and it shall be established unto thee and the light shall shine upon thy ways." Job 22:28 (KJV)

"You shall also decide and decree a thing and it shall be established for you and the light of God's favor shall shine upon your ways." Job 22:28 (AMP)

In context, exegetically speaking, a decree ushers in God's formal and authoritative order from the Highest Court of the Third Heavens into our natural realm. Decrees carry the force of law and command and ordain things to shift and manifest. These decrees are judicial decisions and orders that are irreversible. Decrees cut through circumstances, divide darkness, split mountains, and destroy obstacles to serve an unredeemable sentence on the defeated foes of darkness.

When you decree God's Word, you are bringing things into alignment with the will of the King. I'm talking about a dimension that many believers have never entered into. Most of the church and most believers live out their life of faith in the realm of petition. Most people live and stay in the petition dimension. The "Petition Dimension" is good, but God wants his children to move into the "Decree Dimension" where we are no longer just petitioning God for something to happen, but we are sitting with Him in heavenly places and issuing "Divine Decrees".

In the Decree Dimension, your prayers change from: "Oh Lord, would you help me, God; I need you Lord to help me God. Oh Jesus, God please, Oh God I need you to help me, God please help me with my finances" to powerful decrees, "According to the riches of your glory, send prosperity now. As a child of God, I decree no weapon formed against me and my family shall prosper." This is a whole new dimension! You have the authority according to God's word to decree, "On Earth as it is in Heaven!" and see it manifest right where you are!

Be Sharp!

"Listen, O coastlands to Me, And take heed, you peoples from afar! The Lord has called Me from the womb; From the matrix of My mother He has made mention of My name. And He has made My mouth like a sharp sword; In the shadow of His hand He has hidden Me, And made Me a polished shaft; In His quiver He has hidden Me. And He said to Me, 'You are My servant, O Israel, In whom I will be glorified.'" Isaiah 49:1-3 (NKJV)

As you yield your mouth to the Lord, He will make your mouth sharp. He wants to make your mouth so sharp that when you release decrees, just like Samuel, not one word will fall to the ground. He wants to make your mouth sharp so that every decree that proceeds from your mouth will hit the mark. He said, "My word will accomplish what I send it to accomplish. It will not return unto Me void." He wants to make you a polished shaft. He wants to hide you in the quiver of His House so that when it's time He can pull you out, draw you back and send you to take the gates of the enemy. The sharpness of your mouth comes in the *Selah*. Authority can only flow from intimacy and the revelation of oneness with Christ.

Open your mouth, draw back that bow and decree the Decrees of Heaven. He wants you to see that your words when aligned with Heaven are weapons that will penetrate!

> *"And He raised us up together with Him and made us sit down together [giving us joint seating with Him] in the heavenly sphere [by virtue of our being] in Christ Jesus (the Messiah, the Anointed One)." Ephesians 2:6 (AMP)*

According to Ephesians 2:6, God has raised us up and given us joint seating with Him! From my seat in heavenly places, I look down upon my circumstances and situations. I look down upon my adversaries. I look down upon the enemies of the cross. According to Psalms 2:8, I'm sitting with God and I'm laughing my enemies into derision. Now, as one sitting at the right hand of the Lord, as he sits at the right hand of the Father, I look down and I draw back my bow, I draw back the arrows of **Decrees** and send them forth.

I **decree** this shall happen. I **decree** this comes to an end. I **decree** this shall now be established and shall be in order. Poverty is stricken from my family lineage starting now. I **decree** I'm the head and not the tail. I shall lend and shall not borrow. I **decree** over my family that sickness and disease has moved far from us starting right now with my generation. Diabetes comes to a halt starting right now with my generation. Cancer comes to a halt and I **decree** the **Decree** of the Lord that I am healed by His Stripes. None of these things shall come near me or my house. I release the **Decree** of the Lord. God says, "Come up and sit with me and you will surely see what you **Decree**. You are Kings and Priests. I've put an insignia ring on your hand and whatever you bind on earth is bound in Heaven and whatever you loose on earth is loosed in Heaven. You just have to put your insignia ring on it, stamp it, and **decree** it."

> *"I will declare the decree of the Lord!" Psalms 2:7*

Before you ask for it, **decree** it. We have spent most of our time asking or making petitions. Now is the time to move into the "Decree Dimension"! If I decree it, it's established. If I decree it, I will see it. I have to send something in order to see something. What goes up must come down. The rains of your tomorrow are the decrees of your today. If He's going to do anything on earth, He's going to do it through you and me. We have legal right and authority to decree a thing and see it established. Get God's word on your lips, open the bow of your mouth and launch arrows of decrees. In Luke, when Jesus said, "It is written," He was releasing decrees. So don't just memorize scripture. **Decree** it!

"The potency of prayer hath subdued the strength of fire; it had bridled the rage of lions, hushed anarchy to rest, extinguished wars, appeased elements, expelled demons, burst the chains of death, expanded the gates of heaven, assuaged diseases, repelled frauds, rescued cities from destruction, stayed the sun in its course, and arrested the progress of the thunderbolt." — E. M. Bounds

Escape the Noise

Have you ever been on a plane ride sitting close to a crying baby or unruly child? I know I have! There have been numerous times I have envisioned myself parachuting off a plane or helping someone else to exit safely! My dad, Dr. Charlie Fowler, is a pilot so I grew up on planes. I've also traveled extensively in ministry and missions throughout America and 37 nations. Before my twin daughters, Destiny & Zoë, were two years old, we had taken them on flights to 23 states and to another nation. We learned very early how to travel with children. If you're called to the nations but are afraid to do it with children. You can do it! Here's a mini-checklist for anyone that wants to take flight:

1. "Chewys" such as gummy bears, gum etc. to help their ears on take off and landing and to keep their mouth busy for everyone on the plane!

2. Coloring Books, Toys, Games, iPad.

103

3. Snacks (lots of them!)

4. A little Dramamine, Benadryl or Homeopathic Med prior to boarding never hurts either. (Disclaimer: Please seek doctor's advice.)

5. Most importantly, know this; you are sent! God has you and your children as you step out!

Not too long ago, I was introduced to the wonderful invention of noise canceling headphones. Let me just say, I have been raising a hallelujah ever since! What an invention! I have to take them off to hear when a flight attendant or my family tries to speak. We need noise canceling headphones in the Spirit, too! We need to learn how to escape the noise of life so we can hear His voice more clearly. We must escape the noise of life to come away to be in His presence.

Jesus taught us this by His own example. He would escape the noise and sneak away to pray. He would leave the crowd for an audience of one, His Heavenly Father. Whether it was ascending a mountain, finding a garden or launching out into the deep, Jesus knew how to escape the noise. Let's follow His example. Let's put on our spiritual noise canceling headphones so we can lean in and listen to the heartbeat of His presence. Don't just wait for *Selah* moments, carve out a place for them. The secret place is your oxygen. The secret place is where the table is spread to eat and drink in plenty of Jesus. Escape the noise, and enter into divine communion!

Pause In His Presence

It's time for a Selah Session!

Pause, take some time, and ask the Holy Spirit to help you to steward your schedule. Invite Him to take the lead, and to show you how to yield to His plan.

P.A.U.S.E Principle:

- Presence Centered - Center Yourself In His Presence.

- Abandon Agendas - Abandon your daily routine and wait on the Lord.

- Unleash Passion   - Unleash your passion in Worship and prayer.

- Say it - Say what He Says. Speak the Word aloud. Declare & Decree His Promises.

- Escape the Noise - Put on your spiritual noise canceling headphones & listen for His Voice.

Selah Scriptures:

_____

_____

_____

_____

_____

_____

_____

Pause Prayers:

_____

_____

_____

_____

_____

Pause Promises & Prophecies:

_____

_____

_____

_____

_____

Selah Reflections:

_____

_____

_____

_____

_____

_____

Chapter 7

An Extended Invitation

"The atmosphere of expectancy is the breeding ground of miracles."
—Rod Parsley

The Lord is saying, "I'm in the waiting."

A loud, yelling voice easily draws a crowd. It takes purposeful intention to lean into a gentle whisper. "Shhh, I'm trying to listen." The Lover of our souls wants us to lean into His voice. God is saying to us, "Come away with Me!" His whisper is an invitation into His presence to meet with Him face-to-face. In 1 Kings 19:12, we see that as the Lord was speaking to Elijah, He wasn't in the fire, the earthquake, or in the wind, but He was in the still small voice.

When we want to hear someone speaking, we always lean in. If it's a small child, we bend down low. If it's an elderly person, we come in close. If it's a gifted speaker, we sit on the edge of our seats. The pause is an invitation to wait. It is an invitation to lean in. His voice is sweet. His words are sweeter than honey on a honeycomb. His words are life. They are reviving to the soul. His face is full of light. It outshines the brightest of days.

"But those who wait on the Lord Shall renew their strength; They shall mount up with wings like eagles, They shall run and not be weary, They shall walk and not faint." Isaiah 40:31 (NKJV)

The word 'wait' in Hebrew is 'qavah,' which means "to wait, look for, hope, expect." Waiting isn't passive or idle. Waiting is anticipation and expectation that the One your soul loves is coming. It is waiting because the One your soul loves is about to speak.

"When you are Expecting you'll become expecting!" —Joshua Fowler

Lay your head upon the chest of Jesus, and wait. In this pause, you will sync your heart with His. His heart is beating with love for you. His heart is beating with love for the world. Lean in, wait, and then hang on His every word.

"Although I have much to be grateful for as I look back over my life, I also have many regrets. For one thing, I would speak less and study more, and I would spend more time with my family. I would spend more time in spiritual nurture, seeking to grow closer to God so I could become more like Christ." —Billy Graham

Millions were touched by the life of Billy Graham, yet at the end of His life, he desired to spend less time "doing" and more time "being" with his family and with the Lord. What a beautiful expression and reminder for us to grasp. Encounters with God are not just for Sundays, dynamic worship services, or massive prayer gatherings. If you will pause, God can encounter you right now in this present moment. Give the Lord your day. Give the Lord your tomorrow. Give Him every moment. Wait on Him, seek Him, find Him, and then let your flow from union with Him!

The tendency of man is to get caught up in the whirl of doing, doing, doing. The fast-paced culture around us does it's best to lure us into busyness and distraction. Every billboard, every post, and every show attempts to fashion us into its likeness. What we wear, where we go, who we spend time with, what we invest in, all shaped by the things we behold. However, the posture of our hearts should be to rest, rest, rest in the affection and delight of our Beloved. For the pleasure of God will never draw us into busyness, rather it will continually invite us into His nearness.

For example, my wife, Lisa, is absolutely beautiful. I love spending time with her. Her smile, her accent, and her heart bring joy to my life every day! However, what if when I spent time with her I was on my phone the whole time, taking calls, responding to emails, and scrolling through social media. I could be in the same room as her all day long, but never actually embrace and experience the beauty of who she is. I would be lost in the distractions around me. If I then would try to define our relationship by the amount of our time together, but I never looked into her eyes, or gave her my full attention, I would be denying her of single-hearted, undivided attention. Quantity cannot be the total measuring stick of our relationship. However, if I set my phone aside, and locked eyes with her for an hour, or a few hours on a date, and we engaged in conversation, wouldn't that be of much greater value? If I woke up and looked over at her and told her twenty things I loved about her, wouldn't that make her feel loved? If during the day I stopped to kiss her or hold her hand, wouldn't that draw us closer?

YES.

"Don't come into the presence of God to impress Him with something He gave you!" —Bishop T. D. Jakes

God is not impressed by how much scripture we read. He isn't impressed with how many songs we sing. In actuality, it's impossible to impress God. This perfectionist mentality must be broken, and as a matter of fact, it is broken in the pause. This was the problem with the Pharisees. They attempted to capture God's attention by what they did, instead of recognizing that God is captivated by the hearts of His sons and daughters: who know they belong to Him, imitate Him, and reflect the likeness of His Son in the earth. What did the Lord say over Jesus when the Holy Spirit descended upon Him like a dove? "This is My beloved Son in whom I am well pleased." Waiting on Him leads you to behold Him. As you behold Him, you will become like Him.

The Big Reveal

"It is the glory of God to conceal things, but the glory of kings is to search things out." Proverbs 25:2 (ESV)

It is our glory to seek out the mysteries of God. This is a glorious scavenger hunt where we get to seek out the treasures of God's heart. There is joy in pursuit and exploration. We're wholly satisfied in Him, yet insatiably hungry for more. God has invited us as His closest friends to experience Him in great depths of intimacy. We have barely scratched the surface of our revelation of this infinite God who has invited us into fellowship!

Exodus 33:11a says, "The LORD would speak to Moses face to face, as one speaks to a friend." This is a rarity at this time. Few had access to God in a manner that was face-to-face. Yet Moses, as a friend of God, cried out, "Show me your glory." In this friendship, Moses experienced an intimate place of God, which others didn't get to partake of. What a monumental moment in time. Moses pursued God. Moses chased God. Moses was persistent in His pursuit. The rest of Israel was content in their state of living, yet Moses was willing to climb the mountain. Moses was filled with longing to hear from God, and His longing was of such strength that it carried Him up a mountain in pursuit.

Proverbs 16:26 says, "*A worker's appetite works for him; his mouth urges him on.*" What we are hungry for will place an urgency within us to pursue. If we are hungry for natural food, we will drive a long way to eat it. My son-in-law, Eben, fell in love with my daughter, Destiny, and sold all he had in South Africa and flew across the world to marry her. Desire creates urgency, and urgency creates action! When God conceals matters, it is our glory to seek them out. When zeal, hunger, and longings consume us for more of God, we will experience the mysteries and secrets of God's heart.

"Are you going to be an employee or a bride?" —Michael Koulianos

As amazing as this friendship is with Moses, we have access to an even greater depth of friendship! Ephesians 2:18 says, "For it is through Him that we both have a [direct] way of approach in one Spirit to the Father." There is no more separation; Jews and Gentiles have access to the Father. Second Corinthians 3:10 emphasizes the revelation that the fading glory of Moses has been surpassed by the unfading, permanent glory of the new Covenant through Christ Jesus.

The word for "surpass" here in Greek is 'huperballó,' which means "to throw over or beyond, to run beyond; surpass, excel, exceed, transcend." God took the former glory and with His strong right arm, threw it beyond. The fastest pitch ever recorded in baseball was by Nolan

Ryan at 108 MPH. The right arm of the Lord throwing the former glory greatly outweighs this earthly reality. Not only is this Greek word used here, it's also used to describe His peace, love, and the riches of His grace. God truly is unsearchable, infinite, and far beyond anything we could ever fathom with our finite minds, but God has invited us into a beautiful exploration of His nature, of His beauty, and of His character. We get to spend all of our lives into eternity gazing on the beauty of His holiness.

Psalm 138:6 in The Passion Translation says, "For though you are lofty and exalted, you stoop to embrace the lowly. Yet you keep your distance from those filled with pride." God has extended an invitation for us to abide in His embrace and to dwell in intimate fellowship with Him. As we *Pause in His Presence* and pursue Him, we will dive into the mysteries and secrets of the Lord.

"You will do more in one year if you are really filled with the Holy Ghost than you could do in fifty years apart from Him."
—Smith Wigglesworth

Extended Prophecy

3/31/2020

I heard the Lord say, "Extended. For I have extended an invitation for my children to return to me. In this time I'm giving my people an extension. An Extension of time, An extension of life. An extension of vision. An extension of scope. An extension of faith, an extension of hope. An extension to Preach, an extension to Reach! An extension to Sow, An extension to Reap. An extension to return, an extension to receive. So return to me and receive my extension of mercy and grace" says The Lord.

Set your Sails for The Wind of His Presence!

Growing up one of my favorite jobs was working as a lifeguard on Panama City Beach, Florida. One of the perks of the job was taking people on sailboat rides on a 16' Hobie Cat. There were times the wind was so intense that I could fly the hull for days. Then there were times where it seemed as if there were no wind to be found and we would come to a complete standstill. I learned during these times the valuable skill of what is known as tacking. Tacking is to change course by turning a boat's head into and through the wind. As it is in the natural so it is in the spirit. I believe there are times in our lives that we must face the wind. In our church services, families, marriages, relationships, we need to face the wind! We need to *Pause in His Presence*, face the wind of the Holy Spirit and wait for Him to lead us.

Pause In His Presence

It's time for a Selah Session!

Selah Scriptures:

_____

_____

_____

_____

_____

Pause Prayers:

_____

_____

_____

_____

_____

_____

_____

_____

Pause Promises & Prophecies:

_____

_____

_____

_____

_____

_____

_____

Selah Reflections:

_____

_____

_____

_____

_____

_____

_____

_____

_____

Chapter 8

Messy Worship

Let me preface what I'm about to share with you, I believe in excellence and I know that the Word of God declares in Psalms 33:3, "Sing to Him a new song; Play skillfully with a shout of joy." However, we shouldn't sacrifice the move of the Spirit for excellence. We need to have both the excellence of skilled musicianship and the new "Selah Sounds" and "Songs of the Spirit". I believe in having worship rehearsals and order of services. However, I also believe that like a skilled quarterback reads a defense, there are times the Holy Spirit will call audibles and the leaders must make adjustments to win the game or should I say win souls and lead people into *Close Encounters of the God Kind*!

Thieves case houses and banks to observe the patterns of the owners and weaknesses of their security to learn when to break in. If we apply this same thought, in most churches the enemy knows exactly how and when he can rob many blind. It goes something like this:

- 9am - 9:59 AM - Coffee & Fellowship in the foyer or cafe

- 10am - 10:13 AM - 2 - 3 Praise Songs (Upbeat)

- 10:13-15 AM - Welcome the Newcomers

- 10:15-10:20 AM - Offering

- 10:20-27 AM - 1-2 Worship Songs (slow)

- 10:27-30 AM - Video Announcements

- 10:30-10:55 AM - Sermon

- 10:55-11 AM - Prayer & Dismissal

These times might vary here or there, but for the most part many services are very predictable.

"Compose new melodies that release new praises to the Lord. Play his praises on instruments with the anointing and skill he gives you. Sing and shout with passion; make a spectacular sound of joy—"
Psalms 33:3 (TPT)

How long has it been since you were in a corporate worship experience where the people were so lost in His presence that they went off script and lost track of time? When was the last time you weren't able to predict what happens next at church? When was the last time you heard your worship team go off script and sing a new song and write it as they went? When was the last time you heard a musician interpret the Word of the Lord prophetically? We've exchanged minstrels for musicians and psalmists for performers. We need to return to the pattern of the Heart and House of David and release "Selah Sounds" and songs. Songs that bring deliverance, healing and breakthrough. Songs that aren't just about us, but songs that are for and to Him!

We've had far too many professional, cookie-cut worship services; way too many performances and way too little of His presence. Our services are so overproduced and manmade that there's still no room in "The Inn" for Jesus! Services with pretty preludes and intros, majestic bridges, crescendos and dynamic endings, but little to no "Presence Encounters".

Growing up I remember the presence of God sweeping into the sanctuary and the congregation singing song after song. Often, we would sing songs such as, *"We are Standing on Holy Ground"* and *"Surely the Presence of the Lord is in this Place."*

Many times these songs were led by members of the congregation acapella because the musicians and ministers were all on their faces weeping. I remember singing out with such passion with uplifted hands and hot tears falling down my cheeks. There were nights that many of us had to be carried home and shook under the power of the Holy Spirit with stammering lips and unknown tongues all night long. I long for more of these encounters, don't you? This generation and future generations must have their own encounters in His presence.

Red-Hot Revival of Radical Worship

"Then David danced before the Lord with all his might; and David was wearing a linen ephod. So David and all the house of Israel brought up the ark of the Lord with shouting and with the sound of the trumpet." 2 Sam 6:14-16 (MSG)

I see a red-hot revival of radical worship arising in the nations with people young and old dancing like David danced with all of their might! Sons and daughters dancing violently in their homes, churches, parking lots, streets and fields in wild abandoned love for the Father.

The Fields will be Filled!

Caught up in His presence, Jesus and I went for a walk in the heavens. We were walking over Dallas and He said, "I'm looking for a field!"

I replied, "You're looking for a field?"

Then He said, "You're looking for a field, find Me a field!'

Then again while caught up in His presence, He took me on a walk in the heavens and we walked over Dallas together. He said, "Find me a field." Then He said, "Fill the field with people and I will fill the field with My Glory!"

As we've continued these walks together in the Heavens the Lord has shown me cities all over the world that He's looking for fields to fill with His Glory. These fields will be filled with people worshipping and praying. The young and the old will dance together all day and night for weeks and more at a time. They'll be like "Holy Woodstock" gatherings. The sick will be healed and the oppressed will be set free. Miracles, signs and wonders will be the norm. Those that gather in these fields will be sent from these fields into the harvest fields all over the world and the greatest harvest of souls the world has ever known will be reaped.

A Company of Messy Worshippers are Arising!

A company of "Messy Worshippers" are arsing. They are worshipers who are worshipping like never before. They're entering into new realms of the Spirit, and although some religious and traditional people may not understand what they're doing, the Lord is drawn to it. Like Hannah we must enter into dimensions of "Messy Worship" and "Intense Intercession" and give birth to our prophetic promises! Now is the time to dive deeper and deeper into His presence through "Messy Worship" and "Intense Intercession" so we can give birth to the greatest harvest the world has ever known. Are you hungry for more of The Lord? Are you thirsty for more of His presence? If so it's going to take more "Messy Worship"!

Messy Worship.

You know the kind of worship where you dance like David until you can't dance anymore; sweat dripping from your elbows!

Messy Worship.

You know the kind where your heart is pounding out of your chest faster and faster as you get closer and closer looking into those beautiful eyes of fire.

Messy Worship.

You know the kind where you find yourself in the altar long after service the music has faded, eating carpet in a puddle of tears and snot crying out "more Lord."

Messy Worship.

Yes, you know the kind you don't control, but like the woman with her Alabaster Box, you break it over the Lord's feet and let it run wherever it wants to go.

Messy Worship.

Yes, you know the kind where you can't control the tears and you don't care what you look like after service. All that matters is that you have been with Jesus!

Messy Worship.

You know like when you are all alone in His presence and nothing else matters as you're waiting in bated anticipation to hear just one word from His voice.

Messy Worship.

You know the kind where you can't stand anymore because you feel the weight of His glory pinning you to the floor.

We've got to have more of this! We need more "Messy Worship" both personally and corporately. "Messy Worship" is what it will take to usher His presence into cities and nations. "Messy Worship" and nothing less is what it will take to see *Awakening, Revival and Global Harvest!*

Pause In His Presence

It's time for a Selah Session!

It's time for a Selah Session! Pause In His Presence and Engage in some Messy Worship Right Now! Cry Aloud like Blind Bartimaeus, "J~E~S~U~S", Pray like Hannah, pursue like the Woman with the issue of blood, dance like David. Hold on like Jacob until you encounter His presence in a fresh way!

Selah Scriptures:

Pause Prayers:

_____

_____

_____

_____

_____

_____

Pause Promises & Prophecies:

_____

_____

_____

_____

_____

_____

_____

Selah Reflections:

_____

_____

_____

_____

_____

_____

_____

_____

_____

_____

_____

_____

_____

_____

_____

_____

_____

_____

Chapter 9

Presence People, Pastors, Prophets, Places & Portals

"If the presence of God is in the church, the church will draw the world in. If the presence of God is not in the church, the world will draw the church out." —Charles Finney

Presence People

There is a new breed arising in the earth. A breed I would like to call: "Presence People". "Presence People" will not succumb to the ways of the past and will no longer peacefully coexist with religious traditions of men. "Presence People" are too hungry for more to settle for leftovers of yesterday's manna. They are tired of being pampered and pacified by pastors who are more concerned with people in the seats than they are with God's presence in the building. These "Presence People" will follow "Presence Pastors" and "Presence Leaders".

Presence Pastors

The primary concern of "Presence Pastors" is not attracting more people, it's attracting and hosting more of the presence of the Lord. They aren't worried if someone leaves because of the length of the service or volume of the worship. These "Presence Pastors" have left the pursuit of popularity with mere humanity for the popularity of the Divinity. Although "Presence Pastors" love the people, they are more in love with God. Although they don't want to offend anyone, they are not willing to offend the Holy Spirit to keep from doing so. These "Presence Pastors" don't measure their success by how many people are in the building, but rather by how much of God is in the building and how much of His presence is imparted to the people. They know that if you get enough of His presence in the people, that they will be sent forth by the *Power of His Presence* to transform and awake the world they live in.

Presence Prophets

"God's presence is an irreplaceable incubator for leaders."
—*Lyle Phillips*

Alongside these "Presence Pastors" you will see a new breed of prophet arising to help to build the local church. These prophets refuse to minister out of an old wineskin, gift-centric function and have chosen to be "Presence Centered". If it's not centered around Christ and His presence, birthed from the purity of His presence, they don't want to have anything to do with it. They are not performance based prophets, who people wind up and place a demand upon to prophesy. No, they are "Presence Prophets". These "Presence Prophets" function solely out of the presence of the Lord. Thus, they might not say as much, but when they speak it comes to pass. They aren't concerned with impressing the masses with the quantity of their words, they are concerned with pleasing the Father with their quality of words. When God speaks they speak, and when He doesn't they don't conjure something up for the approval and praises of people. "Presence Prophets" are first and foremost carriers of God's presence. Their primary concern is to host Him well. They want to help bring the people to God, and reveal God to the people.

"As you develop intimacy with God, the supernatural becomes natural." —*Sid Roth*

Like Haggai and Zacharia, "Presence Prophets" come alongside these modern day Zerubbabels (Presence Pastors and Apostles) to build the House of the Lord. They desire more than anything to build a resting place for the presence of the Lord. They do so privately and corporately. Much, if not most, of what these "Presence Prophets" say and do will never be seen or known by people. However, the corridors and courts of Heaven know the voices of these "Presence Prophets" very well. For they spend countless hours *Pausing in His Presence* and making intercession for the Kingdom of God to be made manifest on earth. *Ninety-nine percent*, if not more, of a "Presence Prophet's" ministry is done in private and not in public. However, "Presence Prophets" are called to be like Samuel whose words never fell to the ground. (I Sam 3:19)

Pause In His Presence

It's time for a Selah Session!

Pause In His Presence and declare that from this day forward you will be a person of His presence; your family will be a family of His presence, and your ministry will be a ministry of His Presence.

Selah Scriptures:

_____

_____

_____

_____

_____

_____

_____

_____

_____

_____

_____

_____

_____

Pause Prayers:

_____

_____

_____

_____

_____

_____

_____

Pause Promises & Prophecies:

_____

_____

_____

_____

_____

_____

_____

_____

Selah Reflections:

Presence Places & Portals

"Jacob left Beersheba and went to Haran. He came to a certain place and camped for the night since the sun had set. He took one of the stones there, set it under his head and lay down to sleep. And he dreamed: A stairway was set on the ground and it reached all the way to the sky; angels of God were going up and going down on it. Then God was right before him, saying, 'I am God, the God of Abraham your father and the God of Isaac. I'm giving the ground on which you are sleeping to you and to your descendants. Your descendants will be as the dust of the Earth; they'll stretch from west to east and from north to south. All the families of the Earth will bless themselves in you and your descendants. Yes. I'll stay with you, I'll protect you wherever you go, and I'll bring you back to this very ground. I'll stick with you until I've done everything I promised you.'" Genesis 28:10-15 (MSG)

I see The Lord raising up "Presence Places and Portals" all around the world. Some churches are being transformed into "Presence Centers" and many homes are becoming "Presence Places." These "Presence Centers and Places" aren't centered around a personality, they are presence centered. I see people coming together from all over to *Selah* and entire cities and regions will become "Presence Portals".

Holy Hot Spots

"So continuing daily with one accord in the temple, and breaking bread from house to house, they ate their food with gladness and simplicity of heart" Acts 2:46 (NKJV)

In 2018, I had a prophetic encounter where I saw the Lord raising up "Holy Hot-Spots" all over the world. These "Holy Hot Spots" and "Heavenly Wi-Fi" boosters were not only local churches they were in homes. The people gathered in worship and intercession extending the transmission of the frequency of God's presence in neighborhoods and cities around the world.

No-Fly Zones

"He also brought them out with silver and gold, And there was none feeble among His tribes." Psalms 105:37 (NKJV)

"All the believers were one in mind and heart. Selfishness was not a part of their community, for they shared everything they had with one another. The apostles gave powerful testimonies about the resurrection of the Lord Jesus, and great measures of grace rested upon them all. Some who owned houses or land sold them and brought the proceeds before the apostles to distribute to those without. Not a single person among them was needy."
Acts 4:32-35 (TPT)

The Lord showed me that these "Presence Places" will be "Spiritual No-Fly Zones" where the enemy will not be able to disrupt the work of God or harm His people. Literally sickness or disease will not be able to abide in these presence places. I saw people jumping ditches and running into these churches and homes that had become "Presence Places and Centers". They would come from near and far to beneath the high-speed downloads of heaven in these "Holy Hot-Spots". The Lord said they will travel from all over to be healed and delivered in these "No-Fly Zones". I saw like in Acts 4, These "Presence Centers" will be so blessed that no one will be in lack. I saw like the Children of Israel there will not be one sick or feeble one among us. We are entering into the days that some of God's Generals such as Smith Wigglesworth and Kathryn Kuhlman prophesied of where no sick person would leave without being healed!

We relocated to Dallas, Texas at the word of the Lord, July 20, 2018. That evening I received a prophetic dream. In this dream I went to Heaven I met the Prophet Elisha and a few other people. Then I was granted "Diplomatic Immunity", and I received a heavenly health certificate. I heard the Lord say, "You have a clean bill of health and will pass through territories unscathed and unharmed." He went on to say, "I'm passing out health certificates and granting diplomatic immunity to my prophets, apostles and people." Then The Lord revealed to me how to teach others how to go to heaven to be cleansed and come back healed. On my way back from heaven to earth, I passed by another prophet friend that was ascending into heaven to receive one also. The Lord went on to say that I was going to begin operating a greater healing anointing and flowing in the supernatural. He said, "A New Breed of Healing Evangelists will arise and that Voice of Healing 2.0 was about to begin!"

I believe this word is coming to pass today and we must lay hold of it by faith. I believe it was given to prepare us for the times we are in today. To walk in faith knowing that things such as a "Global Pandemic", Covid-19, viruses and diseases are not able to harm us when we are sent forth with "Kingdom Diplomatic Immunity" and "Heavenly Health Certificates".

On March 11th, 2020 while in prayer the Lord revealed to me that we can wear worship like garments and that it will ward off sickness and disease. He showed me how the aroma of His anointing that we receive during times in His presence is like an "Insect Repellent" that keeps viruses and diseases away from us. Yes, worship is a spiritual insect repellent. Worship is like a "Holy Force Field" that surrounds the life of the worshipper. Wear worship like a garment everyday. Put on the "Perfume of Praise" and let the fragrance of His presence fill every room you walk into! The following is a transcription of the prophetic word that I shared on social media March 13th, 2020:

"I heard the Lord say, "Just like when the Children of Israel's Houses were safe when marked with the blood of the Passover lamb, so shall it be for those who are washed in my blood and marked by My presence. For how much more powerful is the blood of My new covenant? For My blood will never lose its power.

In the coming days there will be what some will say is an uncommon phenomenon. The world will now see a distinguishable difference between those who are carriers of My presence and those who are not. Those who have been washed in my Son's blood and who are marked by my presence will not be harmed.

For the fragrance of my presence will drive out sickness and disease and the aroma of my anointing will destroy every yoke of the enemy. Yes, Christ is the cure for sin and Christ is the cure for every sickness, virus and disease.

Many have asked, "What shall we do?" And I say, Abide in Me. Dwell in my House. Stay close to me, yes, Live in My shadow and nothing shall harm you. Put on the garments of praise, for your praise and worship will be like a supernatural repellent. Yes your worship will ward off viruses. Put on the Lord Jesus Christ. Put on the whole armor of God. Be clothed with my presence. Be Led by My Spirit.

Walk by faith and not by sight. Go when and where I say go and stay when and where I say stay. Declare and decree my Word and it will not return void. Do not fear. For I have not given you a spirit of fear, but of power, and of love and of a sound mind. Receive my peace. Yes, Keep your mind on me and you will remain in my perfect peace. Live in my peace. You will see that this too shall pass.

For in this hour and in the days to come I will send forth many of you who are carriers of my presence and you will drive out the effects of the virus through the victorious sounds of praise and worship. Many will speak my word and healing shall come to many of those who have been infected.

For who am I? I am your Healer. I am your Protector.
Who am I? I am your Defender. I am your Strong Tower.
Who am I? I am your Shelter. I am your Redeemer.
Who am I? I am the Way-Maker. I am your Provider.
Who am I? I am the Prince of Peace.
Who am I? I am He who was dead and yet now lives.
Who am I? I am the King of Kings and Lord of Lords.
Who am I? I am the Lord of Angel Armies and I'm fighting for you.
Who am I? I am the Author and Finisher of your faith.
Who am I? I am your Passover!
Who am I? I Am all that you will ever need and more," declares the Lord.

Garments of Praise

"To console those who mourn in Zion, To give them beauty for ashes, The oil of joy for mourning, The garment of praise for the spirit of heaviness; That they may be called trees of righteousness, The planting of the Lord, that He may be glorified."
Isaiah 61:3 (NKJV)

The House of Obed-Edem - A House of His Presence

"So David would not move the ark of the Lord with him into the City of David; but David took it aside into the house of Obed-Edom the Gittite. The ark of the Lord remained in the house of Obed-Edom the Gittite three months. And the Lord blessed Obed-Edom and all his household. Now it was told King David, saying, 'The Lord has blessed the house of Obed-Edom and all that belongs to him, because of the ark of God.' So David went and brought up the ark of God from the house of Obed-Edom to the City of David with gladness." *2 Samuel 6:10-12 (NKJV)*

When you host the presence of God in your home like Obed-Edem hosted the Ark of the Covenant, you will be blessed. Not only will the Lord bless you but all that belongs to you will be blessed, because of His presence. The question is will you host His presence? Can the Ark of The Covenant take up residence in your home?

The House, The House, The House

"And I also say to you that you are Peter, and on this rock I will build My church, and the gates of Hades shall not prevail against it." Matthew 16:18 (NKJV)

The House of God

Will you host His presence in the House of God? I've been to churches and heard ministers treat God like a guest when He's the "Master of the

House". It's His house! Often, He's treated worse than a guest. We need to give the Lord His house back; to let His presence lead the way.

Your House

Let your home become His dwelling place, too! Fill your house, every corner and square inch of your room with worship and prayer. Give your house back to the Lord afresh and anew. Then your house will be a "Presence Place", "No-Fly Zone" and "Holy HotSpot" for your neighbors to be transformed through.

You are His House

"Have you forgotten that your body is now the sacred temple of the Spirit of Holiness, who lives in you? You don't belong to yourself any longer, for the gift of God, the Holy Spirit, lives inside your sanctuary." 1 Corinthians 6:19-20 (TPT)

"We are like common clay jars that carry this glorious treasure within, so that the extraordinary overflow of power will be seen as God's, not ours." 2 Corinthians 4:7 (TPT)

You are the house or temple of the Holy Spirit. You are His "Jar of Clay" that He is putting on display to reveal His glorious treasure to others. House His presence. Host His presence. Carry His presence. Release His presence. Everywhere you go usher His presence into every room. To every grocery store, every parking lot, school, office, bank, sports event, gym, beach. You are a living love-letter sent from the Lord to those who are in need of Him. Be His house. Some people won't go to church so we must bring His house to them.

- **The House of Stephanas** - We must be addicted to His presence; ministering unto the Lord and others.

"I beseech you, brethren, (ye know the house of Stephanas, that it is the firstfruits of Achaia, and that they have addicted themselves to the ministry of the saints,)" 1 Corinthians 16:15 (KJV)

- **The House of David** - Rebuilding the House of David will usher in revival!

"The key of the house of David I will lay on his shoulder; So he shall open, and no one shall shut; And he shall shut, and no one shall open." Isaiah 22:22 (NKJV)

"On that day I will raise up The tabernacle of David, which has fallen down, And repair its damages; I will raise up its ruins, And rebuild it as in the days of old; That they may possess the remnant of Edom, And all the Gentiles who are called by My name,' Says the Lord who does this thing." Amos 9:11-12 (NKJV)

"After these things I will return to you and raise up the tabernacle of David that has fallen into ruin. I will restore and rebuild what David experienced so that all of humanity will be able to encounter the Lord including the gentiles whom I have called to be my very own,' says the Lord." Acts 15:16-17 (TPT)

- **The House of Peter** - Healing in the house

"By this time they were in front of Peter's house. On entering, Jesus found Peter's mother-in-law sick in bed, burning up with fever. He touched her hand and the fever was gone. No sooner was she up on her feet than she was fixing dinner for him."
Matthew 8:14-15 (MSG)

- **The House of Cornelius** - Household Salvation, Holy Spirit Baptisms, Supernatural Signs & Wonders

"At that time there was a Roman military officer, Cornelius, who was in charge of one hundred men stationed in Caesarea. He was the captain of the Italian regiment, a devout man of extraordinary character who worshiped God and prayed regularly, together with all his family. He also had a heart for the poor and gave generously to help them. One afternoon about three o'clock, he had an open

vision and saw the angel of God appear right in front of him, calling out his name, "Cornelius!" Acts 10: 1-3 (TPT)

"As Peter was in deep thought, trying to interpret the vision, the Spirit said to him, "Go downstairs now, for three men are looking for you. Don't hesitate to go with them,[i] because I have sent them." Acts 10: 19-20 (TPT)

"While Peter was speaking, the Holy Spirit cascaded over all those listening to his message. The Jewish brothers who had accompanied Peter were astounded that the gift of the Holy Spirit was poured out on people who weren't Jews for they heard them speaking in supernaturally given languages and passionately praising God. Peter said, "How could anyone object to these people being baptized? For they have received the Holy Spirit just as we have." So he instructed them to be baptized in the power of the name of Jesus, the Anointed One." Acts 10:44-48 (TPT)

● **The Potter's House** - Houses of Renewal & Reformation

"God told Jeremiah, 'Up on your feet! Go to the potter's house. When you get there, I'll tell you what I have to say.' So I went to the potter's house, and sure enough, the potter was there, working away at his wheel. Whenever the pot the potter was working on turned out badly, as sometimes happens when you are working with clay, the potter would simply start over and use the same clay to make another pot. Then God's Message came to me: 'Can't I do just as this potter does, people of Israel?' God's Decree! 'Watch this potter. In the same way that this potter works his clay, I work on you, people of Israel. At any moment I may decide to pull up a people or a country by the roots and get rid of them. But if they repent of their wicked lives, I will think twice and start over with them. At another time I might decide to plant a people or country, but if they don't cooperate and won't listen to me, I will think again and give up on the plans I had for them.'" Jeremiah 18:1-10 (MSG)

Chapter 10

Prevailing People Live Face to Face

"Whenever, though, they turn to face God as Moses did, God removes the veil and there they are—face-to-face! They suddenly recognize that God is a living, personal presence, not a piece of chiseled stone. And when God is personally present, a living Spirit, that old, constricting legislation is recognized as obsolete. We're free of it! All of us! Nothing between us and God, our faces shining with the brightness of his face. And so we are transfigured much like the Messiah, our lives gradually becoming brighter and more beautiful as God enters our lives and we become like him."
1 Corinthians 3:16-18 (MSG)

Once while *Pausing in His Presence*, the Lord asked me a rhetorical question, "What is My Presence?" Then He said, "My Presence is my Face"! This encounter led me to an exciting time of study and research. I was delighted to find that the most common Hebrew term for "presence" is panim פָּנִים, which is also translated "face," expressing an intimate, close, personal encounter with the Lord. God has invited us into face-to-face friendship. A Jacob generation is arising who will seek God's face and not his hands; a generation who will wrestle and contend for awakening. The man said, "Let me go for the day breaks." (Gen 32:26) but Jacob said, "I will not let you go unless you bless me." We must refuse to be refused and deny to be denied!

Have you ever tried to talk to someone and they were not facing you? When we are truly in His presence we are not just in the same room with Him. We are not just behind him or to the side of Him. He's facing us and we are in His Face. It's time to get in His Face. Yes, it's time for some real Facetime with Daddy God! We must turn our eyes upon Jesus and get in His face.

Turn Your Eyes Upon Jesus
By: Helen Howarth Lemmel
Public Domain

Turn your eyes upon Jesus
Look full in His wonderful face
And the things of earth will grow strangely dim
In the light of His glory and grace

Pray until You Pray Through

When my children were smaller they would run into the room and jump on me in the bed. Sometimes I would act like I was sleeping and they would try to open my eyes and they would grab my face and say, 'Daddy, Daddy, Daddy"! This is what our Abba Father desires for us to do. He wants us to come closer and closer. Where we are face to face, cheek to cheek, heart to heart and it's here in His presence that we are changed into His image from glory to glory!

"For you bring me a continual revelation of resurrection life, the path to the bliss that brings me face-to-face with you."
Psalms 16:11 (TPT)

My grandaddy who preached the gospel for 70 years would often say, "The difference in your generation and my generation is that we prayed until we prayed through, but you pray until you get through. You go to church just to get what you want, but we went and stayed until we met with God. We pray until we pray through." They would pray beneath the stars, sometimes without a tent, and other times they would build a brusharbor with four corner posts, branches and leaves placed across the top seeking Jesus relentlessly night and day. You would hear people for miles praying and interceding that God would save and heal their land.

"They will stand before God, for they seek the pleasure of God's face, the God of Jacob. Pause in His Presence." Psalm 24:6 (TPT)

My grandaddy told me phenomenal stories of hundreds coming in from all over and getting saved in these meetings all because there were a people willing to contend for a move of God. We need to go back to relentless hunger. We need to return to that place where we will pray until we pray through; until we see entire regions running to Jesus.

Press, Persevere & Prevail

Further into the life of Jacob, we see the man he wrestled with ask him, "What is your name?"

He replied, "Jacob."

The man said, "Your name shall no longer be called Jacob, but it shall be called Israel for you have struggled with God and with men and you have prevailed."

Your press and your perseverance is turning into prevail. Glory! Keep pressing, keep persevering then you will prevail. Declare this over yourself today: "I will prevail!"

Your Destiny is in Your Identity

Are you ready for a name change? A name change bursts within as you hold onto God and refuse to let go. Your nature will be changed. Your perception will be changed. Your eyes will awake to see yourself for who God says you are so you can walk in the fullness of God that dwells within you. Peniel in the hebrew means "The Face of God". At the place of Penial, there is a choice: to give way to the flesh or to press through, break through and pray through. This identity change will make alive your destiny. It will lift you higher. The Lord spoke to me recently saying, "I long for the full expression of Myself in you to arise in the earth." God longs for the fullness of who you are as His child to shine on earth. Receive the sealing of His identity in your spirit-man, remove every lid, erase the lines, and arise as His full expression. Be free, undignified, radiating with His life.

Identify with the Power and not your past

You can identify with the past or you can identify with the power. You have the choice: the past or the power. "It's not by might nor by power, but by my Spirit says the Lord." All of us have had a struggle, all of us have been through some hardship, all of us have been called a deceiver, all of us have been called something or been rejected or forgotten or forsook, had people lie about us, cheat us, just things we've been through. God is saying, "No more!" When you receive Christ, that old nature is crucified. Now you're alive in Christ Jesus. How can you move to that place? **Perseverance.** Press through the veil of the flesh. Jacob was in a place of desperation. He was in a place where he had to have God show up. The angel of the Lord actually touched his thigh and his hip went out of socket.

The Word will Keep you Alive

My dad, Dr. Charlie Fowler, had an airplane crash and his hip went out the back of his buttocks and was crushed on the ground. His foot was torn off and his nose was hanging on a thread. He laid in the wreckage of a plane for 15 hours declaring, "I shall not die but live and declare the works of the Lord." We found him the next day and they said there wasn't a vein in his body to give him blood because he had been so brutally taken out from the airplane crash. The Word of the Lord kept him alive. My dad had to have his hip replaced where they put a steel hip in. I've been in the house while my dad has sat in the recliner and his hip went out of socket. Pow! It sounded like a shotgun and everyone in the house could hear it. My dad is a very strong man with the will of 100 men, but he cried in anguish from the excruciating pain. I had never seen my dad like that.

I want you to visualize Jacob wrestling with the angel of the Lord and the angel touched his thigh. When the angel touched it, that hip went out of socket, and the anguish Jacob felt. But the pain didn't stop him from the press. The pain didn't keep him from persevering. He said I've had the pain, but I do not want that old nature anymore. With perseverance, he said, I'm going to hold on until you bless me. The leg was falling out of socket, the anguish, the pain, nerve endings being ripped off. Picture it! I'm going to hold on!

The angel said, "Let me go."

But Jacob said, "I won't let you go!"

Face to Face not Face to Hand

"Heaven's culture is first and foremost Presence focused."
—David Binion

Most of the church relies on a face to hand encounter. They only want what they can get from God's hand. However, a people that will prevail with God, are a people that will press, persevere and pray until they are in the face of God. When you get in a space like Moses, you begin to shine with His glory and His presence.

We are called to live in the place of face-to-face encounters!

"God claims the world as his. Everything and everyone belongs to him! He's the one who pushed back oceans to let the dry ground appear, planting firm foundations for the earth. Who, then, ascends into the presence of the Lord? And who has the privilege of entering into God's Holy Place? Those who are clean—whose works and ways are pure, whose hearts are true and sealed by the truth, those who never deceive, whose words are sure. They will receive the Lord's blessing and righteousness given by the Savior-God. They will stand before God, for they seek the pleasure of God's face, the God of Jacob." Pause in his presence. Psalm 24:1-6 (TPT)

This is Jacob! There is a generation that will be like Jacob that will go for the pineal experience. Be face to face until we are changed into his image from glory to glory. Do you want to be changed from glory to glory?

Unveiled Face

Now you've got my feet on the life path, all radiant from the shining of your face. Ever since you took my hand, I'm on the right way.
Psalms 16:11 (MSG)

How do you go from glory to glory? With an unveiled face, when you see God face to face and when you press through the pineal experience. When you persevere, you move into a place of prevailing and in that place of prevailing there is a release of His presence! It is in this place of His presence that there is a release of His power. His power will manifest in your life. God will release signs and wonders and miracles in and through you: just as Smith Wigglesworth moved in signs and wonders and healings, just as they did in the book of Acts, just as we read about in the epistles, you will begin to become living epistles read upon by men. Portals begin to open up, angels begin to ascend and descend and His glory comes in!

Are you a prevailing person?

If we are going to have hotspots, if we are going to have regions that are on fire that are awakened, there has to be a prevailing people in those regions who will prevail through prayer, praise and prophecy! You have to know how to press in. You can not be a person who waits for the glory to come and just get into it. You need to be a person that will persevere and press on for your entire region to come into the glory! You might feel good, but the rest of the region has to enter into this portal. There has been an expansion of this portal over the region. The expansion comes through a prevailing people. Prevail through prayer, praise and prophecy! Pray it through! Prophecy it through! Praise it through!

Prevailing People are Passionate and not Passive

Prevailing people are not passive or waiting on the defense. Prevailing people are actively in pursuit, warring with the sword of God's Word! Although some have taught us "Don't take a prophetic word and put it upon a shelf, and wait to see if it comes to pass." You must take the prophetic word and judge it. How do you judge the prophetic word? You judge it with the Word of God. If it doesn't line up with the Logos, then it's not a true rhema. Take the word of God and put the prophetic word up beside it and if the prophetic doesn't identify with God's Word, then you judge it as false. How else do you judge a prophetic word? You bring the word before your leadership. Let your leadership judge the word. They can help you to understand timing, just as the sons of Issachar were able to discern the times and the seasons.

Timing is Essential

The biggest mistake that is made is timing. This is why God gives five-fold ministry gifts. Five-fold ministry gifts will help you understand the times and the seasons. They will help you not get ahead of God or lag behind. Every prophecy, every dream, and every vision is subject to be judged. If you receive something and you don't allow somebody to check your work, it can lead to a big mess. Everybody needs accountability with authority. Everyone should have someone that can tell them no. If you don't have someone in your life that can check your work and tell you no, you're in a danger zone!

Don't Take God's Name in Vain

The most common way people take God's name in vain is when they say the Lord said something when He didn't. The fear of the Lord must be restored in the body of Christ to honor what God is truly saying. We cannot slap His name on our opinions and feelings. Don't say the Lord said something when really it is out of the mind, flesh, soul, or carnal desires. God is the same yesterday, today, and forever. His Word is sure and has no fault. We should not be moved by feelings, we should be moved by faith, so if we start feeling led, we have to understand that our feelings will lead us astray.

War with The Word

You are called to war with prophecy. If you get the wrong word and start to use it as a sword, as a ramming rod for your life, it will put you in the wrong place at the wrong time doing the wrong thing. There are a lot of people that proph-a-lie instead of prophesy. It's crucial to have discernment between soul and spirit. However, if you get a word that you know lines up with the Word of God and your leadership has helped you understand the timing, then you can take that word and war with it! You can say, "God, your word declares this. You sent your servants and they exalted over me this and this. I declare this. I decree this. I prevail with this word. I prophecy this word." When you begin to do that, that word will begin to unfold and come to pass.

When I was younger, my parents owned some property in Florida. One day my dad dropped me off at this lot with just a sling blade and a machete then said, "Clear it." I worked for two days until my hands were bleeding and the third day my dad showed up with a crew of men with big tractors and they plowed the rest of the field.

I asked my dad, "Why?"

He said, "I just found them and figured we'll finish it up with them." I mean for days I was swinging and my hands were bleeding, I remember those guys coming up with those tractors and easily plowing everything over. **It's harder to work when your ax is dull.** The enemy will try to blunt your edge with the things you go through. Now, I see this story as a prophetic vision. It's like when God sends His angelic hosts and when we start working with His word! He proclaims, "That is My Word and I'm going to perform My Word! I'm going to send My angels and they will assist you. They will plow everything that you're not able to get out of your way." Get ready! God is sending you reinforcements!

"Now Jacob went out from Beersheba and went toward Haran. So he came to a certain place and stayed there all night, because the sun had set. And he took one of the stones of that place and put it at his head, and he lay down in that place to sleep. Then he dreamed, and behold, a ladder was set up on the earth, and its top

reached to heaven; and there the angels of God were ascending and descending on it. And behold, the Lord stood above it and said: "I am the Lord God of Abraham your father and the God of Isaac; the land on which you lie I will give to you and your descendants. Also your descendants shall be as the dust of the earth; you shall spread abroad to the west and the east, to the north and the south; and in you and in your seed all the families of the earth shall be blessed. Behold, I am with you and will keep[c] you wherever you go, and will bring you back to this land; for I will not leave you until I have done what I have spoken to you." Then Jacob awoke from his sleep and said, "Surely the Lord is in this place, and I did not know it." And he was afraid and said, "How awesome is this place! This is none other than the house of God, and this is the gate of heaven!" Genesis 28:10-17 (NKJV)

Ladders lowered in Cities

Jacob said, "Surely the Lord is in this place and I was unaware of it. How awesome is this place.This is none other than the house of God; the gate of heaven." He then saw a ladder lowered down with angels ascending and descending. I see as the generations of Jacob begin to prevail in America, "Hot Spots", "Holy Hubs", "Houses of Awakening", "Houses of Revival", and entire regions throughout America being awakened night upon night. The sick will be healed, blind eyes are opening, and deaf ears are opening. As prevailing people raise up, I see places that God will raise this decree in the earth.

God lifted me up and showed me things to come. I have seen the day when the average believer will lead 15 people to the Lord in one day. I've seen the day when you will go to your mailbox and someone will come to you and ask, "What must I do to be saved?" I have seen the day when you will go to Walmart and somebody will ask, "What must I do to be saved?" You will go to work and go on break and somebody will ask, "What must I do to be saved?" Churches will have to employ hundreds of people full-time just to handle the harvest and to disciple the people that are coming into the Kingdom.

I've seen the day where people will pull over to the side of the road, fall to the ground crying out to God saying, "The Lord, He is God." The Greatest Awakening the world has ever seen is here. This is not confined to one church, it is going to break out throughout all of America and throughout the nations. Will you be a prevailing person? Will you press? Will you pray? Will you prophecy? Will you praise until you praise through? Will you pray until you pray through? Will you prophecy until you prophecy through?

What do we want? We want more face-to-face encounters. We receive the help of the Lord, we receive His presence, we receive face-to-face encounters.

Selah Grace is Born!

"Behold—here I stand, and the children whom the Lord Yahweh has given me are for signs and wonders in Israel, sent from the Lord Almighty, Commander of Angel Armies, who is enthroned on Mount Zion!" Isaiah 8:18 (TPT)

On the afternoon of September 22nd, 2020 at 5:17pm, a Sign & Wonder was sent from Heaven to Earth. Our bundle of Joy and beautiful baby girl, Selah Grace Fowler, was born weighing 7 lbs and 10 oz and 19". My wife and I truly believe Baby Selah Grace is a prophetic sign of the Grace the Lord has released in the earth to *Selah*. She is a sign that it's time to *Pause in His Presence* and lift up His Word in our lives more than ever before. Her birth is signifying the dawning of a new day of the "More of The Lord" that's available for those who will *Pause* and *Pursue Him*. It's the start of a "Sudden Awakening" where suddenly after suddenly will overtake the earth.

Receive His Divine Grace to *Selah*. Don't strive, *Selah*! Don't settle, *Selah*. Don't sleep through your suddenly. Selah and enter into all that the Lord has for you. Your "Selah Sessions" will usher you and many others into sudden breakthroughs, sudden strategies, sudden connections, sudden favor, sudden opportunities, sudden doors, sudden miracles and healings, sudden signs and wonders, sudden surprises, sudden revival, sudden awakening and sudden harvest.

There's More!

I thought we had reached the conclusion of writing this book. However, recently while ministering at a church I planted in Orlando, Florida, the presence of Lord swooped into the room and I was no longer able to speak. I began to weep uncontrollably as did many people all over the sanctuary. During this time, I received two significant prophetic visions.

Waiting at the Altar

The first was of the Lord standing at the altar as The Bridegroom waiting for His Bride to meet Him. Then I saw the Bride turn and run away. She was running here and there to do the work of the Lord. I heard The Lord say, "Will you meet me at the altar or leave me at the altar?" I began singing this prophetic song, "Will you meet me at the altar?" Then my daughter, Destiny, and I responded as His Bride in song, "We will meet You at the altar; we won't leave You at the altar." I pray this picture is etched into your memory as it has been mine so the next time He invites you to meet Him that you won't leave Him to stand alone, but instead you will *Pause in His Presence* to meet Him at the altar!

The Water of Worship

The second vision was a prophetic vision of the "water of worship". Over the years I've taught and written about worship being like water according to Isaiah 55 and John 4. However, this prophetic vision was so profound that I felt I must include in the book. The Lord showed me the water of worship filling cities so much so that massive bodies of water were forming. I saw Him looking over from heaven and seeing His reflection in these bodies of water. I was reminded of *The Lion King* movie when Simba saw his reflection in the water, He could also see His father's reflection. So it is with us as we worship. Our worship becomes water for the Lord to see Himself in the earth. He's attracted to our worship! Then when we look through the water of our worship we can discover who we are in Him and who He is in us! The time has come for "Presence People" to fill cities all over the world with the water of worship. It is then and only then that The Lord will see His reflection in the earth. Yes, it is then and only then that we will display His image to the world and lay the greatest harvest of all times at His feet.

Over 20 years ago while in an intimate time of worship an anointed minstrel and dear friend, Shonda Anderson, was ministering to the Lord on the keyboard and I began to flow prophetically in song. During this "Selah Session", I spontaneously sang the following song:

Right Here in Your Presence
By: Joshua Fowler & Shonda Anderson

Right here in your presence we wait on You,
Right here in your presence we wait on You,
Lord, we wait on you, lifting Holy hands to You,
Lord we wait on you, we minister unto You,
Right here in your presence, we wait.

I can't think of a better way to conclude this book than for you to stop and do just what the words of this song say. Take a few minutes right now and *Selah. Pause in His Presence* and lift your hands to the Lord. *Pause in His Presence* and minister unto the Lord.

Pause In His Presence

It's time for a Selah Session!

Selah Scriptures:

_____

_____

_____

_____

_____

Pause Prayers:

_____

_____

_____

_____

_____

_____

_____

_____

Pause Promises & Prophecies:

_____

_____

_____

_____

_____

_____

_____

Selah Reflections:

_____

_____

_____

_____

_____

_____

_____

_____

_____

Selah Scriptures & Pause Passages

There are two times to *Selah*. When you feel like it and when you don't! Below are a few "Selah Scriptures" and "Pause Passages" to further unveil the reality that *Selah* is always in season.

When Your Hero Comes to YourRescue, Pause in His Presence!

"My true hero comes to my rescue, for the Lord alone is my Savior. What a feast of favor and bliss he gives his people!"
Psalms 3:8 (TPT) Pause in His presence.

When The King of Glory Appears, Pause in His Presence.

"You ask, 'Who is this King of Glory?' He is the Lord of Victory, armed and ready for battle, the Mighty One, the invincible commander of heaven's hosts! Yes, he is the King of Glory!"
Psalms 24:10 (TPT) Pause in His presence.

In times of Pain, or Spiritual Drought, Pause in His Presence.

"Now I'm reaching out to you, thirsting for you like the dry, cracked ground thirsts for rain." Psalms 143:6 (TPT)
Pause in his presence.

When You Need a Hiding Place, Pause in His Presence.

"Lord, you are my secret hiding place, protecting me from these troubles, surrounding me with songs of gladness! Your joyous shouts of rescue release my breakthrough." Psalms 32:7 (TPT)
Pause in His presence

In Times of Safety & Security, Pause in His Presence.

"We have heard about these wonders, and then we saw them with our own eyes. For this is the city of the Commander of Angel Armies, the city of our God, safe and secure forever!"
Psalms 48:8 (TPT) Pause in His presence.

In times of Faith for Deliverance, Pause in His Presence.

"But I know the loving God will redeem my soul, raising me up from the dark power of death, taking me as his bridal partner."
Pause in His presence. Psalms 49:15 (TPT)

"From heaven he will send a father's help to save me. He will trample down those who trample me. Pause in his presence He will always show me love by his gracious and constant care."
Psalms 57:3 (TPT) Pause in His presence

When You feel Trapped, Pause in His Presence.

"For they have set a trap for me. Frantic fear has me overwhelmed. But look! The very trap they set for me has sprung shut upon themselves instead of me!" Psalms 57:6 (TPT) Pause in His presence

When you need The Lord's help, Pause in His Presence.

"I stand silently to listen for the one I love, waiting as long as it takes for the Lord to rescue me. For God alone has become my Savior. He alone is my safe place; his wrap-around presence always protects me. For he is my champion defender; there's no risk of failure with God. So why would I let worry paralyze me, even when troubles multiply around me? But look at these who want me dead, shouting their vicious threats at me! The moment they discover my weakness they all begin plotting to take me down. Liars, hypocrites, with nothing good to say. All of their energies are spent on moving me from this exalted place. Pause in His

presence I am standing in absolute stillness, silent before the one I love, waiting as long as it takes for him to rescue me. Only God is my Savior, and he will not fail me. For he alone is my safe place. His wrap-around presence always protects me as my champion defender. There's no risk of failure with God! So why would I let worry paralyze me, even when troubles multiply around me? God's glory is all around me! His wrap-around presence is all I need, for the Lord is my Savior, my hero, and my life-giving strength. Join me, everyone! Trust only in God every moment! Tell him all your troubles and pour out your heart-longings to him. Believe me when I tell you—he will help you!"
Psalms 62:1-8 (TPT) Pause in His presence.

When the Enemy falls in the pit, Pause in His Presence.

"The Lord is famous for this: his justice will punish the wicked. While they are digging a pit for others, they are actually setting the terms for their own judgment. They will fall into their own pit." Psalms 9:16 (TPT) Consider the truth of this and pause in His presence.

When you need forgiveness, Pause in His Presence.

"Then I finally admitted to you all my sins, refusing to hide them any longer. I said, 'My life-giving God, I will openly acknowledge my evil actions.' And you forgave me! All at once the guilt of my sin washed away and all my pain disappeared!"
Psalms 32:5 (TPT) Pause in His presence.

In times of Sacrifice and Worship, Pause in His Presence.

"The best I have to bring, I'll throw it all into the fire as the fragrance of my sacrifice ascends unto you." Psalms 66:15 (TPT) Pause in His presence.

When You Ask for His Mercy, Pause in His Presence.

"God, keep us near your mercy-fountain and bless us! And when you look down on us, may your face beam with joy!"
Psalms 67:1 (TPT) Pause in His presence.

When Justice is Revealed, Pause in His Presence.

"Then how glad the nations will be when you are their King. They will sing, they will shout, for you give true justice to the people. Yes! You, Lord, are the shepherd of the nations!"
Psalms 67:4 (TPT) Pause in His presence.

As The Lord goes before to lead you, Pause in His Presence.

"O Lord, it was you who marched in front of your people, leading them through the wasteland." Psalms 68:7 (TPT) Pause in His presence.

During praise and worship, Pause in His Presence!

"Let all the nations of the earth sing songs of praise to almighty God! Go ahead, all you nations—sing your praise to the Lord!"
Psalms 68:32 (TPT) Pause in His presence.

In times of shaking, Pause in His Presence.

"Though I have set the earth firmly on its pillars, I will shake it until it totters and everyone's hearts will tremble."
Psalms 75:3 (TPT) Pause in His presence.

When you wonder where God is, Pause in His Presence.

"As I thought of you I moaned, 'God, where are you?' I'm overwhelmed with despair as I wait for your help to arrive."
Psalms 77:3 (TPT) Pause in His presence.

When the Lord Strikes the Enemy, Pause in His Presence.

"You went forth for the salvation of Your people, For salvation with Your Anointed. You struck the head from the house of the wicked, By laying bare from foundation to neck. Selah"
Habakkuk 3:13 (NKJV) Pause in His presence.

Pause in His Presence, Daily!

"What pleasure fills those who live every day in your temple, enjoying you as they worship in your presence!"
Psalms 84:4 (TPT) Pause in His presence.

About the Authors

Joshua Fowler

Joshua Fowler is a fifth generation preacher, with a rich heritage of ministry. He flows with prophetic precision and apostolic authority. He has been in ministry all of his life and has been preaching the gospel for 33 years. Joshua has ministered in 37 nations as an international conference speaker. He ignites revival and mobilizes strategies to usher awakening into nations and generations.

Joshua is looked to for prophetic coaching. He's a spiritual father to many leaders. Joshua convenes prophetic roundtables called R.O.A.R. = Roundtables Of Awakeners & Revivalists Online & Onsite and leads S.O.A.R. = School Of Awakeners & Revivalists Online and Onsite. Joshua is the author of "Daily Decrees", "Prophetic Praise" and several other anointed books. He's a gifted musician, psalmist and recording artist.

At the outset of the Pandemic, Joshua heard the Lord say "gather My prophets and lead My people in Global Communion." In obedience to this mandate, he and his wife Lisa have gathered the prophets and hundreds of thousands of believers from around the world to join together online to participate in Global Communion.

Joshua is happily married to Lisa. The Lord has blessed him with 5 children and 3 grandchildren. He and his family reside in a suburb of Dallas, Texas and they travel full-time bringing a 'Now Word' to the church. The Lord has given them a mandate to 'Awake The World'.

Zoë Fowler

Zoë Fowler is a 6th generation minister. She has a rich heritage of ministry and has ministered throughout North America, Brazil, Asia, Africa and Europe. The cry of Zoë's heart is first-love pursuit; to lead generations and nations to encounter God's fiery love. Her heart burns with a passion for Jesus that draws many into the presence of God through teaching and worship.

She is a gifted psalmist and minstrel of the Lord. Zoë has released two worship albums, "Stay Awhile" and "Face to Face" and has been featured on many other worship projects. Zoë is a sought after worship leader and anointed prophetic speaker for national and international conferences. She has a heart for her generation, especially for empowering young women to walk in purity and to fulfill their destiny. She's the founder of HeyYoungLady.com where she shares life-changing blogs to empower young ladies. Zoë is a graduate of Christ For The Nations and she is the Worship Minister at Catch The Fire DFW.

Also Available:

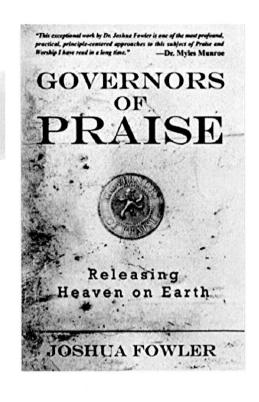

DAILY DECREES FOR ACCESSING ABUNDANCE — DISCOVER THE POWER OF JOB 22

JOSHUA FOWLER

GOVERNORS OF PRAISE — Releasing Heaven on Earth

JOSHUA FOWLER

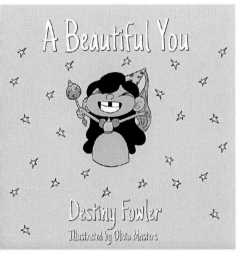

Children's Book

Worship CD

AwakeTheWorld.org

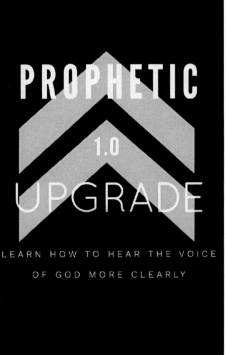

Book, Like & Follow

Joshua Fowler

Speaking Engagements:
DrFowler@me.com
AwakeTheWorld.org

Like & Follow:
Facebook: @drjoshuafowler
Instagram: @thejoshuafowler

Zoë Fowler

Speaking/Worship Engagements:
zoefowler@icloud.com
HeyYoungLady.com

Like & Follow:
Facebook: @zoenoelfowler & @heyyounglady
Instagram: @soundsofzoe & @hey.younglady

Longwood, Florida USA
we bring dreams to life